RATIONALITY AND RELIGIOUS THEISM

Throughout the ages one of the central topics in philosophy of religion has been the rationality of theistic belief. Philosophers and theologians have debated whether it is rational to believe certain propositions about God's existence and nature. This book proposes that parties on both sides of this debate might shift their attention in a different direction, by focusing on the question of whether it is rational to be a religious theist.

Explaining that having theistic beliefs is primarily a cognitive or mental affair but being a religious theist involves a whole way of life that includes, but goes beyond, one's beliefs or cognitive faculties, Golding suggests that to qualify as a religious theist a person must pursue a good relationship with God by following a religious way of life. Utilizing a Pascalian strategy, Golding argues that it can be pragmatically rational to be a religious theist even if the evidence for God's existence is minimal. The argument is applied to the case of Judaism, articulating what is involved in religious Judaism and arguing that it is rationally defensible to be a religious Jew. The book concludes with a discussion of whether a similar argument might be constructed for other versions of religious theism such as Christianity or Islam, or even for non-theistic religions such as Taoism or Buddhism.

Offering a new approach to an ancient topic, whilst also engaging in a discussion of classic and contemporary writings on the rationality of religious commitment, this book provides fresh insights to scholars of philosophy of religion, theology and Jewish studies.

ASHGATE PHILOSOPHY OF RELIGION SERIES

Series Editors

Paul Helm, King's College, University of London, UK
Jerome Gellman, Ben-Gurion University, Beer-Sheva, Israel
Linda Zagzebski, University of Oklahoma, USA

Due to the work of Plantinga, Alston, Swinburne and others, the philosophy of religion is now becoming recognized once again as a mainstream philosophical discipline in which metaphysical, epistemological and moral concepts and arguments are applied to issues of religious belief. The *Ashgate Philosophy of Religion Series* fosters this resurgence of interest by presenting a number of high profile titles spanning many critical debates, and presenting new directions and new perspectives in contemporary research and study. This new series presents books by leading international scholars in the field, providing a platform for their own particular research focus to be presented within a wider contextual framework. Offering accessible, stimulating new contributions to each topic, this series will prove of particular value and interest to academics, graduate, postgraduate and upper-level undergraduate readers world-wide focusing on philosophy, religious studies and theology, sociology or other related fields.

Titles in the series include:

Mystical Experience of God
A Philosophical Inquiry
Jerome Gellman

Religious Diversity
A Philosophical Assessment
David Basinger

Rationality and Religious Theism

JOSHUA L. GOLDING
Bellarmine University, USA

ASHGATE

Published by
Ashgate Publishing Limited
Gower House, Croft Road
Aldershot, Hants
GU11 3HR
England

Ashgate Publishing Company
Suite 420
101 Cherry Street
Burlington, VT 05401–4405
USA

Ashgate website: http://www.ashgate.com

British Library Cataloguing in Publication Data
Golding, Joshua L.
   Rationality and religious theism. – (Ashgate philosophy of religion series)
   1. Theism 2. Rationalism
   I. Title
   211.3

Library of Congress Cataloging-in-Publication Data
Golding, Joshua.
   Rationality and religious theism/Joshua Golding.
      p. cm. – (Ashgate philosophy of religion series)
   Includes bibliographical references and index. (alk. paper)
   1. Judaism–Apologetic works. 2. Philosophy, Jewish.
   3. Jewish way of life. 4. Theism. 5. Religious life.
   6. Religon–Philosophy. I. Title. II. Series.
   BM648.G58 2003
   296.3'5–dc21

                                                                        2002190889

ISBN 0 7546 1567 7 (Hbk)
ISBN 0 7546 1568 5 (Pbk)

This book is printed on acid-free paper

Typeset in Times Roman by Bournemouth Colour Press, Parkstone

Printed and bound in Great Britain by MPG Books Ltd, Bodmin, Cornwall.

Contents

Acknowledgements

Many people and several institutions deserve thanks for helping or enabling me to write this book. Much of this book is based on my doctoral dissertation, which I completed at the University of Pittsburgh in 1989. I would like to thank my director, Nicholas Rescher, as well as my dissertation committee members, Joseph L. Camp, Jr., Tony Edwards, Richard Gale, and Gerry Massey.

Much of the work on this book was done on sabbatical leave during 2000–2001 from my home institution, Bellarmine University, for which I am grateful. I was also fortunate that year to be a research fellow at the Center for Philosophy of Religion at the University of Notre Dame. I would like to thank Alvin Plantinga, Tom Flint, Alasdair MacIntyre, Lynn Joy, David Hemp, Ric Otte, Paul Franks, and Bill Murphy for their valuable suggestions on my work during that time.

Over the years, several colleagues and friends have contributed in one way or another toward this project. In particular, I wish to acknowledge Arie Michelsohn, Peter Vedder, Barry Padgett, Yonah Gewirtz, Jonathan Klein, Victor Schwartz, and David Shatz. From time to time, I have discussed my work with my sisters, Belinda Schwartz and Shulamith Klein. I am also indebted to Linda Zagzebski and Jerome Gellman for their valuable criticisms on earlier drafts of this book.

My wife, Ayala, also read earlier drafts and made helpful suggestions. Of equal importance, she tolerated undue absences from home so that I could work on the book. For this I am very grateful, both to her and my children, Rafi, Rivka, Sammy, Nathaniel, and Vanessa.

Last but certainly not least, I wish to thank my parents, without whose help this book would not have been possible. This book is dedicated to them. One of the most important sections in this book is a discussion of love and respect. If there is anything in that section that makes any sense, I owe it to my mother, Naomi Golding. My debt to my father, Martin P. Golding is equally deep. He has not only been a loving father, but also an intellectual guide and mentor. Needless to say, neither parent takes responsibility for any errors in this book.

JLG

Chapter 1

Introduction

1.1 Overview

Throughout the ages, one of the central topics in the philosophy of religion has been the rationality of theistic belief. Many philosophers and theologians have focused their attention on whether it is rational to believe certain propositions, such as *There is a God, God is eternal, God is omnipotent, God has revealed himself to humans*, and so on. Religious philosophers have advanced arguments in favor of these tenets; skeptics have argued against them. The question of the rationality of theistic belief has been, and will remain, an important topic in the philosophy of religion. Nevertheless, this book proposes that parties on both sides of this debate might shift or at least expand their attention in a different direction.

The guiding thought underlying this book is that there is a difference between *having theistic beliefs* and *being a religious theist*.[1] Whereas *having theistic beliefs* is primarily a cognitive or mental affair, *being a religious theist* involves a whole way of life, that includes, but also goes beyond, one's beliefs or cognitive faculties. In fact, many people are interested in whether it is rational to have theistic beliefs precisely because they think such beliefs play a central role in being a religious person of a certain sort. However, once this distinction is made explicit, it is possible to pose the question directly: *is it rational to be a religious theist?* The aim of this book is to articulate and attempt to answer this question.

This section provides a brief overview of the contents and strategy of this book. The remainder of Chapter 1 covers other introductory material.

Our first task will be to articulate some conception of what is involved in being a "religious theist." Chapter 2 proposes that in order to qualify as a religious theist, a person must *pursue the goal of attaining or maintaining or improving a good relationship with God*.[2] In other words, the religious theist is engaged in a certain kind of spiritual quest. As we unpack this definition, it emerges that in order to be a religious theist, a person must fulfill certain conditions. First, he or she must have *a conception of God*, a *conception of the good relationship with God*, and *a conception of the religious way*, that is, the way to attain (or maintain, or improve) that relationship. In addition, a crucial factor is that the religious theist conceives of the good relationship with God as *supremely valuable* or *qualitatively superior* to any other attainable good. All these notions are addressed in greater detail throughout the course of the book.

1

Chapter 2 argues that in order to be a religious theist in the sense defined, one must have certain *beliefs* about God. However, a key point is that one need not have these beliefs confidently, *but only in a rather minimal way*. In particular, one must believe (a) there is (at least) *a live possibility* that there is a God, and (b) it is *more likely* that one will attain (or maintain, or improve)[3] a good relationship with God by living a religious way of life rather than by not doing so. The notion of a "live possibility" will be elaborated in Chapter 2. Finally, in order to be a religious theist, one must *follow a religious way of life*, that is, one must engage in those actions which one believes increase the probability that one will attain a good relationship with God. Phrased in these terms, the question of whether it is rational to be a religious theist turns out to be not only, and indeed not primarily, a question about the rationality of believing that there is a God, but rather about the rationality of living a certain way of life.

Chapter 3 seeks to describe the conditions under which it is *rationally defensible* to be a religious theist in the sense described in the previous chapter. It will be helpful here to say something about the notion of *rational defensibility* at work in this book.

To say that a position (or a claim, or a way of life) is "rationally defensible" is different from saying that it is "rationally compelling." A position is "rationally compelling" if it can be shown that *any* rational being ought to adopt that position. A position is "rationally defensible" if an argument can be marshaled to support that claim or position, and if criticisms and objections to that argument can be rebutted.[4] However, such an argument might not be compelling upon all rational beings. For example, it might rest on certain assumptions, which are intuitively plausible to some persons but not others. Alternatively, the argument might rest on an appeal to certain experiences, which not everyone has had. In addition, the notion of rational defensibility admits of degrees or comparison. That is, some positions are *more* or *less* rationally defensible than others.[5] Furthermore, some proposition or claim or way of life could be rationally defensible for a restricted or limited group of persons. Now a position is *not* rationally defensible if the denial or opposite of that position has been shown to be rationally compelling.[6] However, as we shall see toward the end of this book, it is possible that two opposing positions could be rationally defensible for different people.

Let us return to the overview of this book. Chapter 3 describes the circumstances under which it would be rationally defensible for a person to fulfill each and all of the conditions that are involved in being a religious theist. A thumbnail sketch of Chapter 3 is as follows. The conceptions of God, the good relationship with God, and the religious way are rationally defensible if they can be articulated in a manner that is *internally coherent*. The notion of God is the central idea underlying theism, and so a considerable portion of the chapter is devoted to articulating this notion. Two different ways of conceiving of God's ontological status are explored.

The relative merits of each of these conceptions are discussed in the Appendix. The chapter also discusses various alternative conceptions of the good relationship with God, and the religious way. It is admitted that not *every* conception of God or the other related conceptions are coherent. However, the argument is made that, in principle, there are coherent ways of articulating these notions.

Chapter 3 continues by proposing that the beliefs that *there is a live possibility that there is a God* and that *it is more likely that one will attain or maintain a good relationship with God by living the religious way of life than by not doing so* are rationally defensible if there is sufficient epistemic justification or evidence for those beliefs.[7] It also discusses the conditions under which there would be sufficient epistemic justification or evidence to support (at least) these minimal beliefs. Since these beliefs are minimal, it is argued that these conditions either are fulfilled, or in principle, could be fulfilled relatively easily. However, whether in fact these conditions are fulfilled depends on certain circumstances to be described in more detail in the chapter.

Next, Chapter 3 proposes that the adoption or maintenance of a theistic religious way of life may be evaluated on pragmatic grounds, that is, on the basis of whether it is potentially more valuable to follow that way of life rather than not to do so. The conclusion is reached that, under certain circumstances, it is rationally defensible to follow a religious way. Stated bluntly, so long as the good relationship with God is plausibly conceived as supremely valuable, and, so long as there is some minimal evidence to believe there is a God and to believe that a certain way of life is more likely than a non-religious way of life to result in that relationship with God, it is pragmatically rational to follow that religious way of life.

Philosophically informed readers will recognize that the pragmatic approach adopted here has roots in what is known as "Pascal's Wager."[8] The reader may wish to view the present argument as an attempt to offer a "neo-Pascalian argument" in defense of the religious life. Nonetheless, there are sharp differences between Pascal's Wager and the present argument. Chapter 3 concludes by showing how the present argument escapes several apparently devastating objections that have been leveled against the Wager. Of course, this does not preclude the possibility that Pascal's Wager might be defended against those objections in other ways.

As stated, the central aim of Chapter 3 is to argue that, under certain conditions, it is rationally defensible to be religious partly on pragmatic grounds, that is, on the grounds that there is a certain great value or potential value to be gained by being religious. But the pragmatic approach may also be used as a guide for how to do philosophical theology, that is, how to work out one's concept of God, the good relationship with God, and related matters. This point requires explanation.

Suppose a theologian is faced with various alternative ways of articulating the notions of God and the good relationship with God. How should she proceed? What strictures are placed on how these concepts are to be worked out? One stricture is coherence. The theologian aims to articulate these notions in a way that is coherent or plausible. Another stricture is the tradition within which a theologian is working. For example, the articulation of a Jewish theology must be based on the texts of the Jewish tradition. However, another stricture might be, *what is the pragmatic consequence of articulating or developing the concept one way rather than the other?* In other words, which articulation of theological notions makes for the potentially most meaningful or valuable conception of what is at stake in being religious? All other things being equal, the conception that provides the more meaningful or valuable understanding of what is at stake in the religious life should be adopted. On the pragmatic approach adopted here, a religious way of life that is potentially more valuable than another way of life is also one that is *more rationally defensible* to choose.

If the argument of Chapter 3 is correct, it turns out that it can be rationally defensible to be a religious theist even if it is *not* rationally defensible to have a full-blown or *confident* belief in God. However, nothing in this book insists that there is no such rationale or that it could not in principle be developed. The conclusion of this book is compatible with the view that such a rationale could be developed, but it is also compatible with the view that no such rationale exists or could ever exist. Further discussion of this point follows later in Chapter 4.

The reader is forewarned that the argument of Chapter 3 is in a deliberate sense unfinished or open-ended. It describes the conditions under which it is rationally defensible to be a religious theist, but it does not insist that these conditions are fulfilled in any particular case. In other words, Chapter 3 deals with the rational defensibility of religious theism in general, but leaves open whether some specific theistic religion, such as Judaism, Christianity, Islam, or another, is rationally defensible. Arguably, in real life there is no such thing as a 'religious theist' in the abstract; rather, there are religious Jews, religious Christians, religious Muslims, and so on. The only way to advance the argument further is to consider a specific brand of religious theism and to ask whether it is rational for some person to be a religious theist of that particular sort. This task is taken up in Chapter 4 with Judaism as an example. The choice of Judaism is based partly on the background and commitments of the author. However, the reader may choose to view the discussion of Judaism as a model for the application of the general strategy pursued in Chapter 3. More on that point follows shortly.

Chapter 4 outlines a conception of what it means to be a religious Jew, and argues that is rationally defensible for some persons to be religious Jews. This involves first an articulation, based on classical Jewish sources, of the Jewish conceptions of God, the good relationship with God, and the religious way. The good relationship with God is conceived in terms of *devekut*, that is, the interpersonal bond between the Jewish people and God. The key notion in the Jewish religious way is that of the Torah, which functions as the central means by which one is supposed to attain a good relationship with God. Chapter 4 argues that in order to be a religious Jew, it is necessary for a person to believe there is at least a *live possibility* that there is a God, and that it is more likely that one will attain a good relationship with God by keeping the Torah rather than by not doing so. We shall also argue that, to be a religious Jew, one must believe there is (at least) a live possibility that certain other doctrines are true.[9] Finally, and perhaps most crucially, in order to qualify as a religious Jew, one must engage in the way of life that is prescribed by the Torah. Applying the general strategy sketched out in the previous chapter, Chapter 4 argues that there is sufficient epistemic justification or evidence for the beliefs that are necessary in order to be a religious Jew, and that it is plausible to conceive of *devekut* with God as supremely valuable. The conclusion follows that it is rationally defensible to be a religious Jew.

While Chapter 4 presents a rational defense of Judaism, it also provokes the question of whether a similar argument could be constructed for other versions of religious theism, such as Christianity or Islam, or even for non-theistic religions such as Taoism or Buddhism. For example, a Christian might adapt the strategy discussed in Chapter 3 by articulating the conditions for being a religious Christian, and then arguing that it is rationally defensible to fulfill those conditions. The question of whether it is *more* rationally defensible to be a religious Jew or a religious Christian would then turn on which of the two arguments succeeds better in its details. Alternatively, perhaps different religious ways of life may be rationally defensible for different persons. At first blush, such a position seems problematic. A different way of stating the problem is by asking whether we can make coherent sense of *religious pluralism*, understood as the thesis that different religions, which make (some) conflicting claims and involve (some) conflicting practices can be rationally defensible for different persons. The concluding section of this book (Section 4.8) responds to this question affirmatively by showing how the approach adopted in this book provides good grounds for adopting a certain form of religious pluralism.

In sum, this book is written from two overlapping perspectives, namely, the general perspective of philosophy of religion, and the more particular perspective of Jewish philosophy. On the one hand, this book offers a rational defense for some form of religious theism. In addition, this book offers a rational defense for being a religious Jew, in a context that allows for religious pluralism.

So much for an overview of this book. At this stage, one final preliminary point needs to be made. In much philosophy of religion, the question about whether it is rational to believe in God is often raised as a question about what is rational for some *individual* person to believe. In this book too, our focus will be on the individual. Nevertheless, the *social* dimension of religion should be borne in mind.

Arguably, the belief in God is not something that an individual has all on one's own, any more than the belief in the latest theory of nuclear physics is something that an individual scientist has on his own. To a large extent, belief is something that *communities* or *groups* have collectively. It could be argued, in Wittgenstein's vein, that individual belief, like private meaning, is *impossible*, and that all belief is inherently social, but we need not go that far here. Often, philosophers of religion ignore this point when they debate arguments about whether it is rational to believe in God. Yet it might very well turn out that what is rational for some group of persons to believe collectively is *not* the same as what is rational for each individual within that group to believe.

Furthermore, when we shift our attention to the question of whether it is rational to *be a religious person*, we should be even more sensitive to the social dimension of religion. For many (if not most) religions, being religious is not really something that an individual does alone. For the biblically based faiths, religion is inherently a social or communal endeavor. This is especially true, for example, in Judaism. One cannot be a "religious Jew" all on one's own; being a religious Jew involves participating in a community of like-minded persons. Hence, ideally, the question about the rational defensibility of being a religious Jew should not be treated as a question about whether some *individual* should make a certain private decision, but rather about whether a certain group of persons should make a collective decision, that is, *to be religious Jews*. This question is less like the question about whether some individual should build a hut or swim across a river, and more like the question about whether a group of persons should build a stadium, form a parliament, or adopt a constitution.

In spite of all this, the main focus of this book is the more traditionally discussed question of whether it is rational for some *individual* to be a religious theist, and in particular, whether it is rational to be a religious Jew. At the same time, there will be no way to avoid completely the social dimension of religion. It will recur continually throughout the course of our discussion.

1.2 Pascal's Wager and the Expected Value Principle

Much of the argument of this book is motivated by critical reflection on the argument known as Pascal's Wager.[10] Blaise Pascal (1623–62) was a Catholic religious thinker, philosopher and mathematician who was working on a philosophical and rhetorical defense of Christianity when he died. The collection of passages he had written were put together and are known as *Pensées* or *Thoughts*, in which the Wager may be found. This argument has a somewhat infamous reputation among many philosophers, though recently there has been a resurgence of sympathetic interest in it. A summary of the Wager runs as follows.

Pascal begins by imagining someone who is faced with the agonizing question of whether he should believe in God or not. Pascal claims that our cognitive abilities are inadequate to determine whether or not God exists. God is infinite, and our intellects are finite. So, the best we can do from an intellectual standpoint is to take a guess about whether God exists or not. However, we are *forced* existentially to make a decision about whether to believe in God. We cannot "remain on the fence." How then should we make this very important decision? Since cognitively we are incapable of making this decision, all we can (and must) do is consider the pragmatic consequences of belief and disbelief. In other words, Pascal proposes that we look at the question of whether to believe in God as primarily a *practical* problem more than a *theoretical* one.[11] We must ask ourselves, what difference does it make to us if we believe, and it turns out that God exists, or does not exist? And, what difference does it make to us if we do *not* believe, and it turns out that God exists, or does not exist?

Pascal continues by asserting that if we believe in God and God exists, we gain infinite bliss or happiness in the next world. Now, if we believe in God and it turns out that God does *not* exist, then the most we have lost is some finite pleasure or good in this world. That finite amount of pleasure or good is what the believer has to sacrifice in order to live the life of a believer. On the other hand, if we do *not* believe in God, we have no chance whatsoever of gaining the infinite bliss of the next world. The best we can do is to gain finite pleasure or good in this world. (Interestingly enough, in the Wager passage Pascal does not explicitly appeal to the notion that the non-believer may suffer punishment in the next world if God does exist.) The situation is very much like that of a gamble or wager. Should we wager on God or not?

Pascal argues that, under these circumstances, the rational choice is to believe in God. In a rather complex and difficult passage, Pascal argues that *a small chance of attaining an infinite value is a "better bet" than a large or definite chance of attaining any finite value*. His underlying assumption is that whenever we are faced with options, it is sensible for us to make a decision by taking into account the potential outcomes of those options, the values of those outcomes, and the probability that those outcomes will occur depending on which option we choose. Contemporary decision theorists have formalized Pascal's procedure by articulating what is known as the Expected Value Principle.[12] For those readers unfamiliar with it, the Principle is best understood by way of example. Suppose I am faced with the following gambling options: Option A: Gamble $1.00 on Horse A; Option B: Gamble $1.00 on Horse B. Suppose I believe that Horse A has a 1/2 chance of winning a payoff of $5.00 (that is, my original dollar returned, plus $4.00); on the other hand, Horse A has a 1/2 chance of losing, that is, incurring a loss of my original $1.00. Further, suppose I believe Horse B has a 1/10 chance of winning at a payoff of $50.00 (that is, my original dollar returned, plus $49.00); also, Horse B has a 9/10 chance of incurring the loss of my original $1.00. Given these options, the Principle works as follows.

For each option, one multiplies the chance of a successful outcome by the positive or negative value of that outcome; one also multiplies the chance of an unsuccessful outcome by the value of that outcome. The results are then added together to obtain what is called the 'expected value' for that option. This seems like a reasonable way of 'weighting' the potential values of a given option against the probabilities that those outcomes will occur. In the case described, the expected value of option A is computed as follows:

$$(1/2 \times \$4.00)^{13} + (1/2 \times -\$1.00) = \$1.50$$

For option B, the expected value would be:

$$(1/10 \times \$49.00) + (9/10 \times -\$1.00) = \$ 4.00$$

Thus, Option B turns out to have the *higher* expected value. According to the Expected Value Principle, the option with the higher expected value is the more rational choice. Hence in this case, the rational choice is option B. Now, according to this Principle, an option that has an extremely valuable possible outcome may turn out to be the rational choice even if the likelihood that that outcome will occur is extremely low. For example, on the basis of this Principle, a gamble on a long-shot horse will turn out to be rational if the payoff on that horse is high enough relative to other available gambles.

Let us now return to the Wager. Pascal has in mind the following scenario: Option A: Believe in God; Option B: Do not believe in God. Again, Pascal claims that the intellect cannot determine whether or not God exists. For the sake of argument suppose the chance that God exists is very small, say 1/100.[14] Furthermore, suppose that if God does not exist, the net gain of belief is zero. This is granting the skeptic quite a lot; arguably, the religious life may have some value even if it turns out God does not exist. In any event, if we assume that value is zero, the expected value of Option A is:

$$1/100 \times \text{infinite value} + 99/100 \times 0 = \text{infinite value}$$

On the other hand, if a person chooses Option B, then, even if God exists, he will not obtain infinite value, and the best he can do is attain some very high finite value by living a pleasant and good secular life. Thus, at the very best, the expected value of Option B is:

$$1/100 \times \text{some finite value} + 99/100 \times \text{some high finite value} = \text{some high finite value}$$

Pascal argues that, given these assumptions, the expected value of belief is infinitely higher than that of disbelief. Hence, the rational choice is to believe in God. Pascal concludes his discussion by considering the practical difficulty of someone who is convinced by the above argument, but finds himself in the sorry state of disbelief. What should such a person do? Pascal recommends basically this: "Act like a believer, speak like a believer, and eventually you will find that you become a believer after all!" Pascal seems to be saying that once a person admits that belief in God is the rational choice, it follows that any means necessary to arrive at a state of belief are legitimate.

So much for a summary of Pascal's argument. There are many objections to Pascal's Wager. We shall state just a few. Whether Pascal had or could have had answers to these objections is not our concern. Later, we shall illustrate how the argument in this book circumvents or avoids these objections.

The first objection concerns Pascal's assertion that one is "forced" to make a decision about whether or not to believe or disbelieve in God. It seems like agnosticism is not only possible, but actual for many people, who quite simply cannot make up their minds about what to believe. We reserve judgment on many questions; why can't the issue of belief in God be one of them? If it is true that the intellect cannot make this decision, then perhaps agnosticism is the best rational response.

Another objection is that Pascal's Wager seems to endorse an ignoble or impious policy of being a religious believer solely out of a desire for self-interest or self-gain. Pascal's Wager focuses on the attainment of "bliss" or "happiness," and his argument seems to be that one maximizes his chances for bliss if one believes in God. But is this an appropriate reason for being a religious believer? Furthermore, assuming Pascal could somehow get around that point, there is separate concern about the moral and intellectual feasibility of generating a belief in oneself in the way Pascal recommends. Suppose that I had somehow convinced you that a certain proposition is in your best interest to believe. Suppose I had even convinced you that you would be morally and spiritually better off if you believed it. Yet, suppose you happen *not* to believe that proposition, for whatever reason. Would it be morally and intellectually feasible to try to inculcate that belief in yourself by using self-brainwashing techniques, such as acting and speaking like a believer? Even if the process worked, would your belief be genuine? And, would it be genuine enough to get you into heaven? Pascal's concluding recommendation seems to involve an insincerity, if not an impossibility.

A third and perhaps more serious problem is that Pascal assumes without argument that *the only possible way of gaining infinite bliss is by believing in God*. Pascal gives no reason for thinking that a belief in God is linked (either conceptually or probabilistically) with the gain of infinite bliss. This gives rise to an objection sometimes known as the problem of "non-standard gods." Pascal seems to ignore the possibility of a non-standard God, such as one that might reward infinite bliss *only* to all those who *disbelieve* him. By what right does Pascal rule out this possibility? This is especially problematic on Pascal's own assumption that our cognitive capacities are limited by our finitude. If God is beyond our finite cognitive abilities to know, perhaps it is impossible to predict what such a being might or might not do to our souls (if we have souls) in the next world (if there is one).

Fourth, Pascal's use of infinite value only exacerbates this problem. By Pascal's own lights, as long as there is even some small chance that one can attain infinite value by being a disbeliever, the expected value of *dis*belief will also be infinite! Even if Pascal has some way of arguing that the chance of attaining the infinite value is *higher* if one believes in God than if one does not, the odd and disturbing result is that both disbelief and belief turn out to have the same expected value, that is, they are both infinite. This point is worth illustrating in some detail.

Earlier we supposed that the chance of attaining infinite bliss if one believes in God and God exists is 1/100. Suppose for the sake of argument that the chance of attaining the infinite value on the option of *dis*belief is much less, say, 1/200. Then, the expected value of disbelief would be:

$$1/\ 200 \times \text{infinite value} + 199/200 \times \text{some high finite value} = \text{infinite value}$$

Stating the same point more broadly, Pascal's strategy seems to rely on the mathematical fact that an infinite value multiplied by even a small fraction will yield an infinite value. But an infinite value multiplied by a *tiny* probability turns out to be equal to an infinite value multiplied by a *high* probability. Some philosophers are inclined to think that this should only make us suspicious of *any* attempt to apply the expected value principle in a case that deals with infinite value. Thus it seems Pascal's Wager is hoist with its own infinite petard.

A final objection concerns what is sometimes called the problem of "other gods." Suppose I am faced with two alternative versions of theism, such that to believe in one is to deny the other. Assuming Pascal's reasoning is correct in all other respects, which version of theism is it rational for me to pick? After all, no matter which one I choose, I may be causing myself to *lose* infinite bliss if the other version turns out to be the right one! Some have argued that noticing this point leads to the result that the most rational thing to do under the circumstances is remain a non-believer after all.[15]

So much for Pascal's Wager and some of its problems. Whether Pascal himself might have had answers to these objections is not our concern in this book. Instead, our aim is to construct a new argument, which utilizes certain aspects of Pascal's Wager but avoids its pitfalls as well. One of the major differences is that this book does *not* endorse a pragmatic justification of *belief in God*. Rather, it offers a pragmatic justification for *living a religious life*, that is, pursuing a good relationship with God, even in the face of doubt about whether there is a God. Furthermore, the approach adopted in this book is not purely pragmatic. To the extent that a minimal belief in God is necessary for living a religious life, this book argues that there is sufficient *evidence* for this minimal belief. Further details of the contrast between

Pascal's Wager and the argument of this book must wait until the end of Chapter 3.

1.3 Motivation for This Project

This book seeks to articulate a rationale for being a religious theist in general, and for being a religious Jew in particular. What is the motivation for seeking a rationale for being a religious theist and for being a religious Jew?

Before describing the motivation, it is necessary to ward off a critical attack. Some religious thinkers are prone to assert either that there is no rationale for being religious, or that it is not appropriate to seek a rationale for being religious. There are various motivations or reasons for these positions.[16] It would take us far afield to address them all. However, some remarks are in order.

To those who simply start off by asserting that there is no rationale, or that there can be no rationale, I beg their indulgence to read through the argument of this book, for if this argument (or any other argument) works, their starting assumption is simply wrong in the first place. On the other hand, to those who say that it is *not appropriate* to seek such a rationale on religious grounds, the question may be asked as to *why* they hold this view. Some might respond that the project of finding a rationale for religious commitment somehow conflicts with what is sometimes referred to as the virtue of faith.[17] It seems that if it could be shown that religious commitment is rationally defensible, that would undermine any role for faith. However, there are several reasons why this objection fails, especially against the strategy at work in this book.

First, even if it can be shown that it is rationally defensible for someone to be religious, there is no guarantee that they *will* be religious; an "act of will" is still required. Analogously, it may be rationally defensible for a married man to remain faithful to his spouse; but that does not guarantee that he will. Temptations of the moment still need to be resisted. Indeed, we do many foolish, wrong things, despite knowing or rationally believing that we should not.[18] Hence, even if a rational defense for religious commitment can be found, that would not necessarily undermine the role of faith.

Second, recall the distinction cited above between what is rationally defensible and rationally compelling. To say that a given choice is rationally defensible does not entail that the choice is devoid of passion, nor does it mean that reason is the *only* factor in the making of this choice. Differently stated, just because a choice is rationally defensible does not mean it is *dictated* or *demanded* by reason. Consider the analogy of a person who is deciding to marry someone. Reason can play a role in helping to determine that a certain person is the right spouse. One can rationally argue, given such and such factors one knows about the potential spouse and about oneself, that this is a "good match." But that does not entail that passion or faith (of some sort) plays no role in this decision. (Perhaps passion or such other non-rational factors can play a role even in a "rationally compelling" belief as well. But whether this is so is not our concern here.)

Third, recall the earlier point that this book does not aim to argue that a *confident belief* in God is rationally defensible. It could very well be that such a thing is beyond the capacity of reason to show. Hence, the approach of this book is compatible with the position that faith or some kind of non-rational or trans-rational commitment must be at work if a confident belief in God is to be obtained.

There is another issue lurking here. Many religious persons think of God as ineffable or indescribable. As a result, some religious individuals are inclined to view any attempt to find a rationale for religious commitment as a violation of God's ineffability. This book takes the ineffability of God very seriously. Indeed, there is a sense in which religious commitment is inexplicable, because God is in some sense inexplicable. But this position can be taken to an extreme. Even if a rational defense for religious commitment can be found, that does not entail that *everything* about God is explicable. This book aims to preserve the notion that God is in some sense ineffable, even in the process of offering a rational defense of religious commitment. Of course, it is up to the reader to judge whether the attempt is successful.

Some religious people might object that any attempt to give a rationale for being religious is "apologetic" in a pejorative sense, for it implicitly admits the *need* for a rational defense. However, this book submits that there is no embarrassment in admitting the desirability for a rationale. The fact that one seeks a rationale does not necessarily entail that one *needs* a rationale in order to maintain one's religious commitment. Analogously, surely it is prudent for someone who is about to get married to consider whether his choice is rationally defensible in the way described above. But this does not entail that if he could *not* provide this rationale, that he should *not* get married to his fiancée. It's just that he is all the more better off, if he can provide this rationale, than if he can't. Having a rationale in hand may crystallize and strengthen his commitment to his fiancée. At the same time, even a person who has such a rationale in hand might legitimately insist that even if he didn't, he would still feel pretty much the same way about his fiancée. And if he did not make this insistence, perhaps we would be suspicious of the depth of his commitment to that person. The same holds for one's religious commitment. Having a rationale in hand may crystallize and strengthen one's choice. This does not entail that the commitment should be put on hold until the rationale is fully articulated.

So far, I have tried to respond to some of the considerations militating against the project of this book. Stated in a more positive fashion, the position underlying the project of this book is that reason can and should play at least some role in all the important decisions of our lives, including the choice about whether to be religious. This position can be defended from two perspectives, namely, what might be called the human perspective, and also from a specifically Jewish perspective as well. By the human perspective, I mean, the universal perspective that we all share as human beings, including religious Jews. By the Jewish perspective, I mean the perspective that flows from traditional Jewish texts, which are not universally shared or revered as sacred texts. These texts include the Hebrew Scriptures and the rabbinic writings, especially the Talmudic literature. Insofar as this book is an exercise in both philosophy of religion and Jewish philosophy, it is fitting to show how the motivation for the project of this book is rooted in both perspectives.

From the human perspective, it is obvious that we are rational creatures, and that, in many contexts at least, reason is a useful tool for helping to decide not only what to believe, but how to live. There is no *a priori* reason to think that this is not true in the case of the choice about whether to be religious. A person who does not at least *consider* whether his or her religious choice (or any other major choice) is rational, is imprudent or foolish. Admittedly, though, if someone says that he wishes to live a foolish life, it is hard to see how any further argument will change his mind.

Incidentally, the pragmatic approach in this book addresses an area regarding religious commitment which is problematic at least for some people, and which is not often addressed in traditional defenses of religious theistic belief. For some, it is not so much that they worry about whether there is good evidence for God's existence. Rather, they do not grasp or appreciate what potential *value* is at stake in having a relationship with God, even if there is a God. Differently stated, they think that religion is unnecessary for living a meaningful and valuable life. Thus, part of our project in this book is to articulate *why it makes sense* to think that a certain kind of relationship with God would be supremely worthwhile. Now, this book does not argue that the *only* way to live a meaningful life is to be a religious theist. However, it does aim to articulate why a theistic religious life is potentially *more* meaningful or *more* valuable[19] than a non-religious life. For people who grasp the great potential value at stake in religion, worries about evidence for God's existence become less bothersome. That is only as it should be, on the approach adopted in this book. Even if there is scant evidence for God's existence, it makes sense to be religious if the potential value of doing so is greater than that of not doing so.

From the Jewish perspective, it can also be argued that it is appropriate to articulate a rationale for being a religious Jew. The sources of traditional Judaism indicate that being a religious Jew is rationally defensible. The Hebrew Scriptures indicate that the religious path or the "way of God," is the way of wisdom and understanding.[20] Surely there are different ways of reading these passages, but the most straightforward interpretation is that they are asserting that the religious path is a rational choice. The rabbinic writings also follow in this vein. The Jewish religious way, that is, the Torah, is considered a form of wisdom.[21] Now it is true that Scripture suggests, and the Talmud teaches that certain things about God and Torah are beyond our understanding, and that we should not even attempt to understand certain things.[22] But this applies to certain particulars, not to being a religious Jew generally.

If the Scriptures and the rabbinic writings indicate that religious Judaism is a rational choice, it is the task of Jewish philosophy and/or theology to articulate that rationale. Throughout the centuries, many Jewish writers have attempted to articulate rationales for believing in God, and for accepting traditional Jewish tenets.[23] The effort to articulate a rationale for being a religious Jew has sometimes been inspired by the need to make a defensive maneuver against skeptical threats launched from outside the Jewish tradition.[24] Indeed, the articulation of a rationale may help a religious person to sort through some crisis in his commitment.[25] However, the effort to articulate a rationale may also be construed as an attempt to articulate authentic Jewish teaching. Some Jewish religious philosophers view it as a religious duty of the highest order.[26]

As mentioned at the outset, the main concern among such writers has been the effort to rationally defend certain traditional Jewish tenets or *beliefs*. The approach here focuses more holistically on the rationality of *being a religious Jew*. Nevertheless, this book is intended as a contribution to the rationalistic endeavor in Jewish philosophy.

Notes

1   This book develops and expands upon a strategy articulated in previous work. See Joshua L. Golding, "On the Rationality of Being Religious," in E. Radcliffe and J. White eds, *Faith in Theory and Practice: Essays on Justifying Religious Belief* (Chicago: Open Court, 1993), and "The Rational Defensibility of Being a Traditional Religious Jew" in *Religious Studies*, vol. 35 (December 1999) pp. 391–423.

2   It might be thought better to define a religious person as one who pursues the goal of attaining *and* maintaining *and* improving a good relationship with God. However, use of the disjunctive term "or" makes clear that on the present proposal, a person counts as religious so long as he falls into any one of these categories. More on this point later. See end of Section 2.2.

3   Henceforward, in general, this cumbersome expression will be dropped for the sake of brevity.

4   In order for a person to have a rationally defensible belief or claim or way of life, he need not be able to defend it *himself*. He may *defer* to someone else (for example, a religious authority or a philosopher) who can. See further discussion below in Sections 2.2 and 3.1.

5   See Section 3.1 for further discussion of the notion of *degrees* of rational defensibility.

6   Another possible category is that of the "rationally permissible." One might say that a position is rationally permissible for a person if and only if its negation is not rationally compelling. However, it need not be one for which an argument can be marshaled at all. Many philosophers hold that it can be epistemically legitimate for a person to hold a position for which no argument can be marshaled, so long as its negation is not

rationally compelling. For a discussion of this in the context of religious belief, see Alvin Plantinga, "Reason and Belief in God" in *Faith and Rationality* (Notre Dame: University of Notre Dame Press, 1983).

7   Chapter 3 does not make the "evidentialist" claim that the *only* way for such (minimal) beliefs to be rationally defensible is if there is (some) evidence for those propositions. Rather, the claim is that *one* way such (minimal) beliefs could be rationally defensible is if there is (some) evidence for those propositions. On evidentialism, see the classic articles by W.K. Clifford, "The Ethics of Belief" and William James' response, "The Will to Believe." Both may be found in M. Peterson et. al., eds, *Philosophy of Religion: Selected Readings* (Oxford: Oxford University Press, 2001).

8   On Pascal's Wager, see note 10 below.

9   See below, Section 4.6.

10   Pascal's Wager occurs in *Pensées*. For a more complete summary and evaluation of the Wager, see Joshua L. Golding, "Pascal's Wager" (see note 1 above). For recent discussions of Pascal's Wager, see Jeff Jordan, ed., *Gambling on God: Essays on Pascal's Wager* (Lanham: Rowman and Littlefield Publishers, 1994).

11   Pascal's pragmatic approach to the question of whether it is rational to believe in God appears to have been a genuine innovation. However, some scholars have claimed there are precursors of Pascal's Wager. See Miguel Asín Palacios, *Los Precedentes Musalmanes del Pari di Pascal* (Santander, 1921). This historical matter is not our concern here.

12   For a general treatment of decision theory, see Richard Jeffrey, *The Logic of Decision* (Chicago: University of Chicago Press, 1983).

13   The positive value of winning this gamble is actually $4.00, not $5.00, since one of the dollars is just a returned dollar, not a dollar that is "won." Similarly for Option B, the positive value of winning is actually $49.00, not $50.00.

14   Actually, Pascal seems to claim that since the intellect cannot determine whether God exists, the probability that God exists is $1/2$. There is a scholarly controversy about whether he makes this claim, and if he did, whether it is legitimate. For discussion of this see Golding, "Pascal's Wager," p. 127.

15   See Michael Martin, "Pascal's Wager as an Argument for Not Believing in God" in *Religious Studies*, vol. 19 (1983) pp. 57–64.

16   See the discussion by Terence Penelhum in *Faith* (New York: Macmillan, 1989) pp. 1–4.

17   On the virtue of faith, see Robert Merrihew Adams, *The Virtue of Faith and other essays in Philosophical Theology* (New York: Oxford University Press, 1987). The present book does not attempt to work out a notion of faith. However, for a notion of faith that dovetails with the argument of the present book, see Joshua L. Golding, "Toward a Pragmatic Conception of Religious Faith" in *Faith and Philosophy*, vol. 7 no. 4 (October 1990).

18   Some philosophers think "weakness of the will" is impossible. On this topic, see William Charlton, *Weakness of Will* (Oxford: Basil Blackwell, 1988). If weakness of will is impossible, a rational defense of religious commitment seems to entail there is no room for the virtue of faith. However, religious philosophers in theistic traditions generally *accept* the possibility of weakness of the will.

19   This book does not aim to explicate the notion of spiritual joy or bliss or pleasure at stake in having a good relationship with God. It is to be admitted that an articulation of this notion would enhance the argument of this book.

20   See, for example, Deuteronomy 4:5–6, Isaiah 33:6, Proverbs 1:7, 2:6, 9:10, Psalms 111:10, Job 28:28.

21   The rabbis identify Torah with wisdom (*chochmah*) or understanding (*binah*) in many passages. See *Midrash Tanchumah* (Warsaw edn) Genesis 1; *Mechilta de-rabbi Yishmael, Yitro* 10; *Shmot Rabbah* 5:5; *Vayikra Rabbah* 11:3. According to *Tractate Berachot* 17a, the purpose or end of wisdom is "repentance and good deeds," that is,

observance of Torah. Sin is viewed as folly in *Tractate Sotah* 3a and *Tractate Sanhedrin* 106a.

22   See *Tractate Chaggigah* 11b, on certain kinds of metaphysical speculation that are considered off limits. In some rabbinic literature, the explanation of the commandment for the Red Heifer (*Numbers* 19) is treated as an example of that which defies human comprehension. See *Bamidbar Rabbah* (Vilna ed.) 19:3 and *Midrash Tanchumah* (Buber ed.) *Chukat* 15.

23   Two classic examples are Moses Maimonides, *Guide to the Perplexed*, and Judah Ha-levi, *The Kuzari*.

24   Remarks in the Introduction to the *Guide for the Perplexed* (Chicago: University of Chicago Press, 1963) p. 5, indicate that Maimonides wrote the *Guide* to alleviate perplexity regarding traditional Jewish doctrines stemming from study of (Aristotelian) philosophy.

25   However, it is also true that from the Jewish perspective, there may be a danger that a person who engages in reflection on whether there is a rationale for being religious may become even *less* committed than he was before. On this topic, see Norman Lamm, "Faith and Doubt" in *Faith and Doubt: Studies in Jewish Thought* (New York: Ktav, 1972) and Joshua L. Golding's critical review of Lamm, "Faith and Doubt Reconsidered" in *Tradition: A Journal of Orthodox Jewish Thought,* vol. 26 no. 3 (Spring 1992), pp. 33–48.

26   See Saadiah Gaon, *Book of Beliefs and Opinions*, trans. S. Rosenblatt (New Haven: Yale University Press, 1951), Introduction: Section VI; Maimonides, *Guide for the Perplexed*, I:50, p.111. Maimonides claims that ideally, belief in God should be based on rational comprehension or argument. See also *Guide*, III:27, pp. 510–512.

Chapter 2

The Religious Theist

2.1 Who Counts as a "Religious Theist"?

In order to investigate the question at issue in this book, we must articulate a conception of the "religious theist." This in itself is an important, though somewhat neglected, topic in philosophy of religion. We shall also discuss the question of what *beliefs* a person must have in order to be a religious theist. The issue of whether it is rationally defensible to be a religious theist is not the aim of this chapter. One should hardly expect that one's conception of what it is to be a religious theist should entail that it is rational to be one. On the contrary, the definition of the religious theist should *leave open* the possibility that there are some *irrational* religious theists. In Chapter 3, we shall address the question of whether it is *rationally defensible* to be a religious theist. However, as we shall see, there are some commitments which a person must have in order to qualify as a religious theist altogether. These commitments follow from the definition of the religious theist. One purpose of the present part is to identify those commitments.

Obviously, there are different ways one might articulate the notion of the "religious theist." Different people have something different in mind when they use this phrase. For the purpose of this book, we shall conceive of the religious theist in a certain way. As a first approximation, a "religious theist" is a person who engages in a certain kind of spiritual quest. More specifically, a religious theist is a *person who strives to attain, or maintain, or improve, a certain kind of good relationship with God*. On this definition, a religious theist is defined not primarily by whether he or she has certain *beliefs*, but by whether he or she *pursues a certain goal*. Let us clarify, expand, and unpack this definition.

Our proposal treats the "religious theist" as someone who adheres to a religion in which the notion of God plays a central role. As I shall argue in more detail later, a person can be a religious theist in this sense even if he *lacks* a confident belief in God. Now it is true that, in common usage, the term "theist" often connotes a person who has a *confident belief* in God. In this book, we are using the term "theist" in a looser sense. A theist is someone who is committed to a theistic way of life, whether or not he has confident theistic beliefs.[1]

The notion of "pursuing a goal" requires comment. Some philosophers are willing to use this locution in a context where it is fully acknowledged (even by the pursuer of the goal himself) that the attainment or maintenance of the goal is impossible, and that the goal is, to borrow Kantian terminology, a "regulative ideal" which will never be attained.[2] For example, in this sense, an athlete might be said to "pursue the goal" of running a mile in one minute. In this case, the athlete might acknowledge that he does not really intend to bring about this goal; rather, he acts "as if" he were intending to do so. However, as used in this book, the phrase "to pursue a goal" is *to make an intentional or conscious effort to help bring it about that some state of affairs – the state of affairs described by the goal itself – is attained or maintained.* The religious theist does *not* view the goal of having a good relationship with God as a mere regulative ideal; he views it as a potential or actual state of affairs, which he seeks to attain or maintain in "real time." Of course, there might be some people who *do* view the relationship with God solely as a regulative ideal. They do not count as "religious theists" in the sense intended here.

We may also make another distinction. Some people pursue the goal of a good relationship with God "for its own sake." That is, they view this goal as intrinsically valuable or worthy of being attained. We may refer to such individuals as *devout* religious persons. However, some religious theists pursue the religious goal not as an end in itself, but for some ulterior motive. For example, a person might be "religious" because that is what is customary in her culture, and she does not want to be censured or punished. Such persons are not devout. On the definition proposed here, a person would still count as "religious" so long as she pursues the good relationship with God, even though her motive is ulterior. Needless to say, it is possible for the same person to have mixed motives for being religious; in which case, she is somewhat devout and somewhat less than devout.

2.2 The Religious Theist's Conceptions

Our definition of the religious theist implies that he or she must *have some conception of God.* Surely, anyone who pursues some goal must have some conception of what is involved in that goal. In this context, to "have a conception of God" means more than just to have some idea in one's mind. To have a conception of God is to have an idea that fits into a nexus of concepts that constitutes a framework for living a certain way of life. Furthermore, there is a difference between *thinking that some conception is coherent* and *having a certain conception.* For example, I might think that the Hindu conception of Ultimate Reality as Atman is coherent, but that doesn't mean I *have* that conception of ultimate reality. As we shall see, to actually *have* a conception of God is, in part, to have certain ideas about what makes something *better* than something else. That will carry implications about how one is inclined to behave. In other words, conceptions of God, and the good relationship with God are *value-laden.* So, to have a conception of God is, among other things, to be committed to a certain notion of what is valuable.[3]

The degree to which a conception or a framework of related concepts is developed or articulated in the mind of the religious theist may vary from one person to the next. But one must have at least some rudimentary conception of God, in order to be engaged in the pursuit of a relationship with God. For the purpose of this book, it is necessary to place some stricture on the conception of "God," so that the definition of the religious theist is not so broad as to be devoid of content. To use a somewhat absurd example, we would not want to allow that someone counts as a "religious theist," just because he happens to use the word "God" to refer to some object or person (for example, one's spouse?) with whom he strives to attain some "good relationship." In short, we need some rudimentary explication of the conception of God in order to give substance to this initial definition of the religious theist. On the other hand, we cannot be too specific about what this term means if we want our definition to cover a wide range of persons.

The hallmark of theism is the notion that God is conceived as *supreme* or *superior* to any other possible being or reality, and at the same time as having *rational agency* or *personhood*.[4] In virtue of his personhood, God is capable of choosing, knowing, and also capable of adopting certain cognitive attitudes such as love and respect. Also, God can, if he chooses, communicate with other persons and entertain interpersonal relationships with other persons. Precisely what all this means may be a matter of debate among theologians and philosophers of religion. For the present, it suffices to say that here God is conceived as the *Supreme Person*. Accordingly, the religious theist is someone who seeks to attain or maintain a certain relationship with God, conceived as the Supreme Person.

We shall turn to a more critical analysis and discussion of the conception of God in Section 3.2. However, one additional point is worth mentioning here. Ordinary religious persons are not always equipped to articulate their concept of God in any great detail. Nevertheless, an ordinary religious theist within a given religious community may *defer* to an authority for further articulation of his theological conceptions. For example, if an ordinary Christian is asked to articulate his concept of God, he might begin by saying something like, God is the Supreme Person. Asked to explain this in more detail, he might defer to some religious authority, that is, a theologian or philosopher of religion. In this case, we may say that he conceives of God (by deferral) in the way that the authority does. The rational defensibility of his conception of God will then be derivative from or dependent upon the rational defensibility of the more detailed conception possessed by that authority.[5] We shall return to this point in the next chapter.

It follows from our initial definition that the religious theist must also have some conception of the good relationship with God. The details of what constitutes that relationship may be more or less developed, and may vary from one theistic religion to the next; but there must be some conception of that relationship at work in order for it to be pursued as a goal.

However, what is crucial for the present purpose is that the religious theist conceives of the good relationship with God as *supremely valuable*. That is, he thinks of the good at stake in having that relationship with God as superior to any other kind of good which he might possibly obtain. Thus, on the present account, to have a conception of the good relationship with God is more than just to have a certain idea in one's mind. It is also to subscribe to a certain notion of what is valuable, indeed, supremely valuable, to obtain.

This holds true even for a religious theist who is not devout in the sense defined above. Even if a person pursues the good relationship with God for ulterior motives, he still counts as a religious theist if he conceives of it as supremely valuable.

It is also possible for someone to think of the good relationship with God in such a way that there can be varying *degrees* of the extent to which one has that relationship. Precisely what this means, and whether it makes sense to have such a conception is a question to which we shall turn in the next part. And, again, with regard to the articulation of this concept in more detail, the same point about "deference" to an authority made earlier holds here as well. An ordinary religious person need not be able to articulate his conception of the good relationship with God in any detail, if he defers to someone who can.

It might be objected that our definition of the religious theist is too exclusive for the following reason. Consider a person who sincerely and confidently believes it is his duty to engage in what he believes to be certain divinely ordained activities. This person engages in these actions strictly because *he thinks it is his duty to do so.* Surely, he should count as a "religious theist." But isn't it conceivable that such a person might *not* be trying to attain any relationship with God? Absurdly, it seems this person would turn out *not* to be a religious theist on the proposed definition!

However, on reflection, this person is indeed striving to attain a certain "good relationship" with God. Such a person conceives of the "good relationship with God" as one in which he fulfills divinely ordained duty. The objection reads too much into the term "relationship." Alternatively, substitute "*right* relationship" for "*good* relationship" in the definition and this case is covered or included by the proposed definition. The individual described aims to have the "right relationship" with God, that is, one in which he fulfills his divinely ordained duty. Therefore, he counts as a "religious theist" for the purpose of this book.

Another objection could be made that we have built too much into the notion of the religious theist by requiring that he conceive of the relationship with God as "supremely valuable." Shouldn't a person qualify as a "religious theist" even if he conceives of the good relationship with God as a kind of good that is just like one good among many others? Obviously, such a person is "religious" in some sense. But it would be quite non-standard for someone to be called a "religious theist" if indeed he thinks that the end goal of his religion is just as valuable as non-religious goods. If he thinks that having a good relationship with God is just as good, or of the same order of goodness as, for example, having money, we would be entitled to say that his status as a "religious theist" is in question.

Finally, anyone who pursues a goal needs to have some idea of *how* that goal is to be pursued. Hence, in addition to having conceptions of God and the good relationship with God, the religious person must also have *some conception of the religious way*, that is, the *way* in which that relationship is to be pursued. In fact, the conception of the religious way and the conception of the religious goal need not be sharply separable. In many religions, the *way* and the *end* are integrally connected. As we shall see later, the religious way might be conceived in such a fashion that it is not just a means to the religious end, but rather as part of the end itself. In any case, the religious way generally includes certain positive and negative actions, that is, "do's and don'ts." It may include physical actions, mental actions, and verbal actions; it may include cultivating certain character traits and avoiding or rooting out others. How one determines or arrives at a religious way is yet another matter to which we shall turn later.

Given our conception of the religious theist, does anything follow about what she might think about conceptions of the "supreme reality" or "supreme being" *other than her own*? What might she think about other conceptions of God? What might she think about other conceptions of the good relationship God, or of the religious way? What might she think of non-theistic conceptions of how to live one's life? At this stage, our answer is simple. To qualify as a religious theist, she need not even have an opinion about such other conceptions. But we shall return to this issue in subsequent chapters.

Our definition of the religious theist is broad enough to include at least three categories of persons. Category I includes those who do not at all believe that they have attained the good relationship with God, and who consider themselves to be seeking to attain that relationship. Category II includes those who very confidently believe (or perhaps, deem themselves to *know*) they have already attained a good relationship with God, and who seek to maintain or improve that relationship. Finally, Category III includes those who fall somewhere between Categories I and II. This includes people who believe, but without much confidence, that they have attained a good relationship with God, and who are trying to maintain or improve that relationship. Of course, it is possible for someone to fluctuate from one category to the other, at different times in one's life. With these distinctions in hand, we are now in a position to ask whether a person must believe in the reality or existence of God in order to be a religious theist.

2.3 The Religious Theist's Beliefs

Clearly, it is possible for someone to be a religious theist, even if there is no God. Of course, if there is no God, then the goal of the religious theist is a chimera; if there is no God, no one can have any relationship with him. A more subtle issue is whether a person must *believe* there is a God in order to be a religious theist in the sense defined above. More generally, our question is to what beliefs[6] is a religious theist committed? First, let us briefly discuss the notions of *belief* and *commitment to a belief*.

For the present purpose, we may say that a belief involves both a *psychological* and a *pragmatic* component. "To believe that *p*" is to have a psychological conviction or a *feeling* that *p* is true. Precisely what is the nature of this conviction is a psychological matter that is not our intention here to explain. Here we take for granted that humans have the ability not only to have convictions, but also to have convictions with different levels of confidence, ranging from weak, to moderate, very strong, maximum or "total conviction." However, a belief is not merely a matter of one's inner psychological state. A person who believes that *p* is disposed to take *p* into account when deciding how to act; he is disposed to consider the implications which *p* might have on his behavior, and to guide his actions accordingly. This brief account of belief will suffice for the present purpose.

Next, let us clarify what is meant by a *commitment to a belief*. Assume that a person engages in some practice *P* in the effort to attain goal *G*. We shall say that such a person is committed to a belief *B* if it can be shown to this person that it makes sense to engage in *P* as a means for *G* only if he has belief *B*. For example, if I engage in the practice of rescuing a lost sailor at sea by flying over the waters in an airplane, I am committed to the belief that a) there is some chance the sailor is still alive and that b) the method of flying over the waters has some chance of success at finding the sailor. For if there is no chance the sailor is alive or no chance that this method will succeed, it does not make sense to engage in this action as a means of finding the sailor.

Let us return to our initial question. To what beliefs is a religious theist committed? The answer is complicated by the distinction between three categories mentioned above. Let us focus initially on Category I, namely, those who do *not* believe they have attained a good relationship with God, and who consider themselves as attempting to attain that relationship.

It is quite ordinary for a person to pursue some goal while being uncertain that conditions are such that he will definitely succeed in attaining that goal. As in the example just given, one need not be confident that the sailor is alive in order to pursue the goal of saving him. Similarly, a person who pursues the attainment of a relationship with God is not thereby committed to having a confident belief in the reality of God. Nevertheless, it seems that such a person is rationally committed to what might be called a "minimal belief" that there is a God, that is, the belief that there is (at least) a *live possibility* that there is a God. Most readers will agree intuitively with this claim. However, it will not hurt to provide a more formal defense.

First we must clarify the notion of a belief that *there is a live possibility that p*. Like any other belief, the belief that *there is a live possibility that p* involves both a psychological and a pragmatic component. The psychological component may be stated negatively: to believe there is a live possibility that *p* is to *not* be in the position of being totally convinced or fully confident that not-*p* is true (or that *p* is false). The pragmatic component may be stated positively: to believe there is a live possibility that *p* is to be disposed at least under some hypothetical circumstances to take *p* into account when deciding how to act. Someone who is *never* willing under any hypothetical circumstances to take *p* into account when deciding how to act does not believe there is a live possibility that *p*.

We may now defend the claim that a person in Category I is committed to having a minimal belief that there is a God. Plainly, a religious theist who pursues the attainment of a good relationship with God realizes that he can attain this relationship only if there is a God. Now, it would be nonsensical, if not psychologically impossible, to pursue this goal if one were psychologically convinced that there is no God. For, to do so would be to attempt to bring about that which one believes one cannot bring about, no matter what one does. Furthermore, it would be irrational to pursue this goal and at the same time never be disposed, under any circumstances whatsoever, to take into account the practical implications of the proposition, *There is a God*. Put simply, a person who is disposed never to take into account the implications this proposition has on his behavior is either a highly confused and irrational religious theist, or is not a religious theist at all. Thus, a person who pursues the attainment of a good relationship with God is committed to the belief that *there is a live possibility that there is a God*.

Are there any other beliefs to which such a religious theist is committed? We have already said that the religious theist must have some conception of the *way* to go about pursuing the attainment or maintenance of a good relationship with God. In fact, he must have more than a *conception* of the way; he must have some *belief* that the religious way which he follows promotes the probability that he will attain that relationship with God. For, if he believes that any action is *as likely as any other* to bring about that relationship, then his religiosity will be empty or vapid; no matter what he does, he will be promoting that relationship equally well. For example, a person who believed that doing good works (whatever that amounts to) is just as likely to promote a good relationship with God as *not* doing good works cannot be said to pursue the good relationship with God *by doing good works*. In order to qualify as a religious theist, a person must have at least some beliefs about what actions (or inactions) promote the attainment of the religious end-goal. It is worth emphasizing that a religious theist is *not* committed to the belief that his religious way has a very high chance of succeeding, or even a chance of more than half. All he needs to believe is that the probability that he will attain the relationship with God is *higher* if he does certain actions rather than others.

Earlier we asked what attitude the religious theist might take regarding alternative conceptions of God other than his own. Here the question may be asked, what beliefs is the religious theist in Category I committed to regarding *alternative religious ways*, that is, religious ways of life that he is aware of but does not follow? In fact, he may very well be in the position of believing that several religious ways are equally likely to promote the good relationship with God as he conceives it. He may very well believe that other religious ways are more likely than his own to promote a *different* kind of 'good relationship with God' as conceived by some *other* religion. Or, he might be in the position of being very confident that his own religious way is the best of all available alternatives. However, what is crucial is that he believes there is a live possibility that *his* religious way will work successfully *for him*, and that it is more likely that *he* will succeed in attaining his goal by following that religious way than by doing nothing. We shall return to this issue in subsequent chapters.

Next, let us consider religious theists in Category II. Such persons regard themselves as pursuing the goal of *maintaining* a good relationship with God. To what beliefs is such a person committed? Obviously, if a person is confident that he has already attained a good relationship with God, it follows that this person must have a confident belief that there is a God.[7] There may also be other beliefs to which he is committed, given his belief that he has a good relationship with God, together with his conception of that relationship. Furthermore, given that he confidently considers himself to be pursuing the goal of maintaining his relationship with God, he must believe that by following a certain religious way, it is (at least) slightly more likely that he will maintain that relationship. In this last regard, he is much like the person in Category I.

Finally, let us consider Category III, namely, those religious theists who have a less than confident belief that they have attained a good relationship with God. Such a person need not have a confident belief that there is a God. A person who has only a minimal belief that he has attained a good relationship with God, may very well have only a minimal belief that there is a God. Of course, a person in Category III might *happen* to be someone who has a confident belief *that there is a God*, coupled with a less than confident belief *that he has a good relationship with God*. In any case, all persons in Category III are committed to believe there is (at least) a live possibility that there is a God and that certain actions rather than others promote the probability that the good relationship with God will be attained and/or maintained.

Our discussion has illustrated some complexities involved in identifying those beliefs to which a religious theist is rationally committed. However, it is safe to conclude that *all* religious theists are committed to the belief that *there is (at least) a live possibility that there is a God* and that *a certain religious way promotes (at least slightly) the probability of the attainment and/or maintenance of a good relationship with God.*[8] Additionally, note that if a person is rationally committed to some belief, he is also committed to any belief that is a logical consequence thereof. Precisely what are those consequences will depend on the details of one's conception of God, the good relationship with God, and one's beliefs about how to attain or maintain the good relationship with God. We shall return to these points later.

2.4 The Religious Theist's Actions

In order to count as a religious theist, it is not enough to have certain conceptions and beliefs about God and the good relationship with God. Most crucially, the religious theist is someone who follows the religious way of life, that is, he does (or avoids) those actions which he or she believes make it more (or less) likely that the religious end goal will be attained or maintained.

Obviously, different persons can pursue the same goal with a different degree of zeal. Furthermore, one individual can pursue the same goal with different degrees of zeal at different times in one's life. Let us say that a person is more religious (or less religious) to the extent that he pursues (or fails to pursue) the good relationship with God. We may also say that a very religious person subordinates all activities in life to the religious goal. Such a person pursues a good relationship with God at every turn, wherever and whenever possible. In any case, to qualify as religious, one need not be "very" religious. Rather, one is "religious" to the extent that one pursues the stated goal.

We may summarize Chapter 2 as follows. A person is a religious theist if and only if:

1 He has a conception of God (as Supreme Person).
2 He has a conception of the good relationship with God (as supremely valuable).
3 He has a conception of the religious way, that is, the way to attain or maintain that relationship.
4 He believes there is (at least) a *live possibility* that there is a God.
5 He believes that following that religious way promotes (at least slightly) the probability that he will attain or maintain a good relationship with God.
6 He follows that religious way.

In Chapter 3, we will consider under what circumstances it is rationally defensible to be a religious theist in this sense.

Notes

1 Readers who think the term "religious theist" should be reserved to apply *only* to those persons who have a fully confident belief in God are invited to substitute some other phrase such as "theistically oriented religious person" wherever the phrase "religious theist" occurs henceforward in this book. Additionally, they may take the aim of this book to consider whether it is rationally defensible to be a "theistically oriented religious person."

2 For a defense of the view that it can make sense to pursue a goal one knows is not attainable, see Nicholas Rescher, *Ethical Idealism: An Inquiry into the Nature and Function of Ideals* (Berkeley: University of California Press, 1987).

3 We shall return to this point at some length in the next part. See Section 3.2 for discussion of whether value judgments are rationally defensible.

4 See Chapter 3, note 4.

5 Arguably, this is much the same way in which an ordinary person may be said to have a conception of, say, an electron or quark. As a non-scientist, my conception of a quark is rather limited. If asked to give details on what a quark might be, I would hastily defer to a scientific authority. The rational defensibility of my belief that there is such a thing as a quark would depend on the ability of the scientist to provide such a rational defense.

6 The question dealt with here is what *existential* and *empirical* beliefs a person must have in order to be religious. Certain beliefs are already presupposed in what preceded, such as, beliefs having to do with one's conception of God, and beliefs about what is supremely valuable. For example, the religious person believes such things as "if God exists, he is the supreme person." In other words, he has beliefs about what a supreme person is like. But these are not *existential* or *empirical* beliefs.

7 In fact, depending on one's conception of the good relationship with God, it may be that such a person must consider himself to *know* there is a God. For, according to some conceptions, the good relationship with God includes having *knowledge* of God. See the discussion below in Section 3.3.

8 This conclusion is based on the generic definition of the religious theist proposed at the outset of this part. With regard to a particular religion such as Judaism, some might object that to qualify as a religious Jew, one doesn't need even these minimal beliefs. Alternatively, other students of Judaism might object that these minimal beliefs are insufficient, and that one needs to have some confident beliefs in order to count as a religious Jew. These objections are discussed below in Section 4.5.

Chapter 3

The Rationality of Being a Religious Theist

3.1 General Remarks

The aim of this chapter is to address the question of whether it is rationally defensible to be a religious theist. For those who are not already religious theists, the question is whether it is rationally defensible to become religious theists; for those who are already religious theists, the question is whether it is rationally defensible to continue as such.

Arguably, there is no such thing as a "generic" religious theist. Instead, there are adherents of particular theistic religions (Judaism, Christianity, Islam, and so on). At the same time, it is undeniable that all theistic religions have certain features in common. In asking whether it is rational to be a religious theist, one might have two different questions in mind. One question is whether it is more rationally defensible to be an adherent of *some* theistic religion *rather than none at all*. Another question is whether it is more rationally defensible to be an adherent of *some particular* theistic religion rather than *some other particular* theistic religion. Our aim in this chapter is primarily to address the former question. However, along the way we shall have things to say that bear on the latter question as well.

It would be impossible to consider, for each and every variety of religious theism, whether it is more rationally defensible to be an adherent than not. Instead, this chapter sets out to describe the circumstances under which it would be more rationally defensible for a person to be an adherent of some theistic religion rather than none. This chapter also argues that, to a large extent, those circumstances are either in fact fulfilled, or in principle, easily fulfilled. However, we shall also find that to some extent, the question of whether or not those circumstances are fulfilled depends on factors pertaining to a given person and to the details of the particular version of religious theism that he or she adopts (or is considering adopting). Thus, the rationale given in this chapter is, in a very deliberate sense, partial or unfinished. To provide a more definitive rationale, one must consider a particular version of religious theism, in connection with a particular person in a particular set of circumstances. That will be the topic of Chapter 4, with Judaism taken as an example.

Let us restate our definition from the end of the last chapter. A person is a religious theist if and only if:

1 He has a conception of God (as Supreme Person).
2 He has a conception of the good relationship with God (as supremely valuable).
3 He has a conception of the religious way, that is, the way to attain or maintain that relationship.
4 He believes there is (at least) a *live possibility* that there is a God.
5 He believes that following that religious way promotes (at least slightly) the probability that he will attain or maintain a good relationship with God.
6 He follows that religious way.

In this chapter, we shall describe the circumstances under which it is rationally defensible for some person to fill each and all of these conditions. In doing so, we must articulate these notions with a logical rigor that goes beyond what was achieved in the previous part, where our concern had been only to outline a conception of what it means to be a religious person. Each of the remaining sections in this part is devoted to one of the above six conditions.

Conditions 1, 2, and 3 state that the religious theist *has certain conceptions*. As stated earlier, to have a conception is not to have some isolated idea, but rather to have some idea which fits into a nexus of related ideas that provides a framework for living a certain way of life. It also involves having certain value commitments. Under what circumstances is it rationally defensible to have a certain conception?

The following seems plausible. It is rationally defensible for a given person to have a certain conception if it can be articulated in a manner that is internally logically coherent, and if other related concepts that the person has also can be articulated in a manner that forms a logically coherent framework. So, a person's conceptions of *God, the good relationship with God*, and *the religious way* may be evaluated by examining whether those conceptions can be articulated in a manner which is internally coherent. This should not be taken to mean that the ordinary (non-philosophically sophisticated) religious person must be able *himself* to articulate these concepts in order for it to be rational for him to have that concept. Rather, these concepts must be articulated by someone (such as a theologian or religious philosopher) to whom the ordinary religious person defers on such matters. Thus, the rational defensibility of the ordinary religious person's theological conceptions will depend upon the ability of the authority to whom he defers for its articulation.[1]

As indicated earlier, the religious theist is in fact committed to something *stronger* than that his concepts of God, and so on form a coherent framework. As stated in Condition 4, he must believe there is at least a *live possibility* that there is a God. Roughly speaking, this means he not only has the idea of God, but also that he believes there is a live possibility that there is a God. Later we shall discuss the circumstances under which this belief is rationally defensible. Our first concern is to articulate the theistic conceptual framework in a coherent manner. However, even at this stage, Condition 4 will be in the back of our minds. We shall return to this point shortly.

The notion of rational *defensibility* is, so to speak, a relative term. One conceptual framework (or claim, or belief, or way of life) can be *more* rationally defensible than another. Also, a given conceptual framework can be *somewhat* rationally defensible, *moderately* rationally defensible, or *very* rationally defensible. The more articulated the framework is in a logically coherent manner, the more rationally defensible it is. One reason for this is that, while some idea may seem coherent on its face, there may be reasons for suspecting that the idea may turn out to be incoherent on further analysis. In addition, while some isolated idea may be internally coherent, it may turn out to be incoherent with other related notions that a given person has. Hence, the more one fully articulates a given framework, the more conceptually plausible that framework becomes. In this chapter, we shall offer a sketch of the theistic conceptual framework. Needless to say, not every theist will agree with the framework as sketched here. Additionally, we shall leave open much room for developing these notions in more detail. How these details are to be filled in may be a legitimate area for debate among theologians.

Over the years, many philosophers have tried to argue that the notion of God and related notions are in one way or another incoherent. To a large extent, attacks on the coherency of the notion of God tend to focus on specific, detailed conceptions of God, which may indeed be incoherent. By the same token, it is difficult or perhaps impossible to provide a *proof* that some concept or conceptual framework is internally coherent. All one can do is articulate that framework in a way that seems coherent, and then field challenges to the coherency of that framework as they arise.

3.2 The Conception of God: The Supreme Person

In this section we focus on the notion of God. Our aim is to articulate this concept, drawing freely on the classic and contemporary sources of philosophical theology.[2] But first, something must be said regarding *how* the concept of God is formed. Theoretically, a concept of God could be formed on the basis of experience (veridical or illusionary; ordinary or "religious"); or on the basis of imagination, fantasy, reading the Bible, reading myths, and so on. It could be formed through some sort of *a priori* process, that is, pure thought or reason (if there is such a thing). Or, it could be formed through some combination of reason and experience. Yet, the historical genesis of a concept is irrelevant to the discussion of whether it is *coherent*. Hence in articulating the concept of God below it is not necessary to discuss its genesis. Such considerations are more relevant to the question of whether a belief that there is a God is rationally defensible. For example, if the concept of God was derived from a veridical experience rather than an illusionary one, that will be relevant to the issue of whether the belief in God is rationally defensible. The issue of the genesis of the concept of God will be more pertinent later when we turn to Condition 4.

Some people mistakenly assume that any attempt to articulate the notion of God is an attempt to say that everything about the notion of God is easy to grasp or fully explicable. This is not correct. It is useful to make a distinction between 1) a logical incoherency, 2) a paradox or something that seems to be logically incoherent at first blush, and, 3) a mystery, that is, something that is unknown or unexplained. An example of a logical incoherency is the idea of a *round square*. Such a thing is impossible. On the other hand, an example of a paradox might be the old saw, "the more you know, the more you know how little you know." Though it seems self-contradictory at first glance, this statement is true. Finally, an example of a mystery might be something that we just don't know or can't know, such as, what is the cause of cancer or, what will the world be like three billion years from now. Another example of a mystery might be how certain people seem to do things that are totally out of character, in a way that we cannot explain. In what follows, our goal is to articulate the notion of God in a logically coherent manner. However, we shall still preserve a substantial sense in which the idea of God is both paradoxical and mysterious.

The notion of God as a Supreme Person does not suffer from an obvious internal contradiction, as does, for example, the notion of a "round square." However, a given person can fail to hold a conception rationally if that person also holds some other related conception, which logically conflicts with the first conception. For example, one's conception of God as the Supreme Person might logically conflict with one's conception of good and evil. Suppose for instance that one maintains both the notion of God as the "Supreme Person" yet at the same time one conceives of that which is impersonal as *better* than that which is personal. Such an individual fails to hold his conception of God rationally. There is no guarantee that a given individual's conception of God is held consistently, for this depends on the details of his conception of God and on his other related conceptions. Thus, even if we can succeed here in articulating the concept of God coherently, that does not guarantee that *everyone* who has this concept holds it coherently.

Given that there may be alternative ways of articulating a certain concept or set of concepts in a logically coherent manner, the question arises whether there are any criteria for preferring one logically coherent articulation of the theistic framework to another. Aside from logical coherency, one can judge an articulation of the theistic framework by reference to certain accepted or revered religious texts, such as the Bible (and/or Talmud and/or Church fathers, and so on) and/or against certain respected, classic philosophical texts (Maimonides, Aquinas, and so on). Obviously, which texts count as respected will be to some extent a matter of religious and cultural background. One can also judge an articulation against certain people's "raw intuitions." Surely, our raw intuitions are shaped by our religious and cultural background. Nevertheless, these are legitimate ways of evaluating an articulation of the concept of God.

Moreover, in evaluating a given articulation of a concept, one might also take into consideration a) its potential explanatory value, b) the *a priori* likeliness of its being provable or at least confirmable in some way, and c) its potential pragmatic value. For example, one should ask questions such as: does a given articulation of a conception of God pose certain puzzles or issues that seem insurmountable? Is one conception of God less "ontologically committed" than another? Given a certain conception of God, how hard will it be to prove or confirm the existence or reality of such a God? In what way does a given articulation of the conception of God make a pragmatic difference to the *value* of being religious or not? This last question makes sense especially in the context of this book, which endorses a pragmatic approach to the rational defensibility of being religious. We may refer to the following as the "pragmatic criterion" for preferring one conception of God over another: *Given two ways of articulating the concept of God that are otherwise equally adequate, one should prefer an articulation which offers more meaning or value to the religious life than the other.* For, as we shall illustrate later, if there is more *potential value* at stake in conceiving of God one way rather than another, then, all other things being equal, it will turn out to be *more rationally defensible* to be religious under the first concept of God than the second.[3]

Now, the core idea we started out with is the notion of God as Supreme Person.[4] What does it mean to think of God as *supreme*? One way would be to think of God as *the absolutely perfect being*, that is, a being who has all perfections, that is, all perfectly good qualities or properties,[5] and absolutely no deficiency. Another way would be to understand God as a being that is "infinitely perfect" or "infinitely good." We may refer to either of these views as *perfectionist* conceptions of God. What motivation is there for thinking of God this way? Based on the pragmatic criterion mentioned above, one might argue that the perfectionist concept of God should be preferred on the grounds that only a perfect being would (potentially) provide the best value for the religious person. Putting the point coarsely, it could be argued that the more valuable one's God is, the more valuable is the potential value of having a relationship with God.

The notion that there is a pragmatic motivation for thinking of God as the most *valuable* being or reality possible makes sense, and it is one we shall endorse later on. However, arguments have been made against the coherence of the *perfectionist* conception of God.[6] Without entering into or passing judgment on such arguments, here we shall take God's supremacy to mean that God is conceived as *qualitatively superior to any other logically possible being or reality*.[7] In other words, God is better *in kind* than any other logically possible being or reality. Roughly stated, even if the goodness in all beings or realities other than God were somehow to be combined, their goodness would not equal or even approach God's goodness. God's goodness is *transcendent*. But this does not necessarily imply that God is *absolutely perfect*. It is rather that God's goodness is, so to speak, on a radically different plane than that of any other possible kind of reality. Exactly what God's goodness amounts to, and what makes God qualitatively superior is an issue to which we shall turn shortly. The relevant point here is that this conception avoids certain problems, which plague the perfectionist concept of God.

Moreover, we shall argue later that so long as God is conceived as the *best logically possible* being or reality, the argument of this book will still go through that (assuming certain conditions are fulfilled) it is more rationally defensible to be a religious theist than not to be one.[8] In effect this will show that even by appeal to the pragmatic criterion for concept selection, there is nothing gained by insisting on the perfectionist conception of God's supremacy. For it will *still* turn out to be rationally defensible to be a religious theist, even if God is *not* conceived as perfect but only as the best logically possible being or reality.

The notion of God as qualitatively superior allows (but does not imply that) God does not have all perfections. It allows (but does not imply) that God has some deficiencies. It also allows (but does not imply) that God *could be better than He is now*.[9] It even allows that God's goodness may increase (or decrease) from time to time, at least in some respect, though perhaps not all respects. What this conception does *not* allow is that there could be some being other than God that is qualitatively just as good as or better than God himself.

In any case, the religious theist must face the following question. What constitutes God's supreme goodness or qualitative superiority? In other words, by virtue of having what features or properties[10] is God conceived as *qualitatively supreme*? Second, is it *coherent* to think that having certain properties rather than others renders God "qualitatively supreme"? Third, assuming that the notion of God is coherent, we may ask whether there is some positive reason the theist can give to *motivate* his notion that having certain properties rather than others renders God supreme. This latter question raises a more general philosophical question, namely, whether it is rationally defensible to consider certain properties *better* than others. It is very difficult, perhaps impossible, to prove to everyone's satisfaction that certain properties are better than others. All the religious theist can do is articulate coherently those features which he thinks make for a supreme reality, and then try to explain what motivates the religious theist to think those features are indeed so special.

Traditionally, there are basically three related ways in which God is conceived as better *in kind* than any other possible being or reality. First, God is conceived as *metaphysically* superior. Second, God is conceived as *volitionally and intellectually* superior. Third, God is conceived as *morally* superior, or superior in character. In each case, God's superiority is a matter of *kind*, not *degree*. Precisely how these three aspects are related will itself be part of our discussion. Let us articulate each of these notions in more detail.

God's Metaphysical Superiority

God is conceived as the primal, foundational, and ultimate being or reality. God's supremacy involves a certain set of *metaphysical* features or properties. These features are "metaphysical" in that they pertain to God's very being or reality, that is, God's "essence." They pertain to God as he is in himself, so to speak, and not insofar as he interacts with other things. Classically, such features include (at least) *necessary being* or *reality, independence, uncreatedness, eternality*, and *uniqueness*.[11] The notion that God's existence or reality is *necessary* is that by his very nature, God must exist or be real. Precisely what it is about God's nature that makes his being or reality necessary is left open here; though we shall have some comment on this issue later. The notion of *independence* is that God does not depend for his existence or reality on anything outside himself. This follows logically from God's essential necessity. Since God exists or is real by his own nature, there is nothing external upon which his existence or reality depends. It also follows from his necessity that God is *uncreated* (had no origin in time) and *eternal* (cannot possibly pass out of existence or reality). A necessary reality could not have begun to be at some point in the past, nor could it ever go out of existence. Finally, God is necessarily one or *unique*. God is of the sort that there can only be one of his kind. Exactly in what sense this is so may be left open for the present purpose.[12]

In addition, here we shall classify as a "metaphysical" property God's power or capacity to be the *causal source* or *condition of being* or *explanatory ground* for all other possible things. Some philosophers might hesitate to classify this as a metaphysical property, because it seems impossible to describe this property without referring to the possibility of there being something *other* than God. As such, this property does not pertain strictly and solely to God's essence or nature itself, apart from his relations with other things. Nevertheless, we may still treat this as a "metaphysical" feature in a certain sense. For the theist, even if it were the case that God had not created or continually sustained the world, God would still have had the power or capacity to do so. Speaking roughly, there is something about God's essence, which allows God to be the causal source or condition of being for all things. Hence, we may classify this as a metaphysical property in the sense that it pertains to God's being or reality, despite the fact that in order to describe it, we must make reference to possible things other than God.

The above list is not intended as an exhaustive list of God's metaphysical properties or features. Arguably, there are other features that belong on this list. For example, there are some features, which may follow logically from those already stated (for example, that God is incorporeal). On the other hand, other properties are more controversial. One such feature is *simplicity*. Some wish to conceive of God's essence as simple or non-composite. Yet others find that this notion is too restrictive. Two more examples of this sort are *immutability* and *impassibility*. Roughly, immutability means "not subject to change" and "impassibility" means "not being affected by anyone or anything external." At first glance, it may appear that these notions are incompatible with the notion of personhood. This is one reason the theist may resist ascribing these properties to God. We will return to this issue later. In any case, the present point is that the above list is open to further development.

The notion of a reality that is necessary, independent, eternal, uncreated, unique and which has the power to be the cause or ground of all else does not contain any obvious logical incoherency (though we shall consider one objection later). Furthermore, it is easy to see that the difference between a being or reality that has such properties and a being or reality which does not have them is not a matter of *degree* but a matter of *kind*. The difference between a reality that is necessary, eternal, and independent as opposed to one that is contingent, mortal, and dependent is a radical one. The former is conceived not just as one that will live a lot longer, is less likely to pass away, and so on. Similarly, if one being or reality has the capacity to be the cause or ground of all else, the difference in power between such a reality and everything else is one of kind, not degree.

We may turn then to the motivational question: *why* might the religious theist think that having such properties or features make for a metaphysically *superior* reality? Some philosophers think that ultimately there is no way to defend rationally a view about why someone considers something valuable. If this view is correct, the theist might respond that *he just does* find these traits to be better than their opposites. In this case, the theist is no worse off, rationally, for having his conception of God than anyone else who has any value commitments. For, if our value commitments are in principle not rationally defensible, then presumably they are not subject to criticism either.[13]

Alternatively, the religious theist might claim that we have learned through religious experience that there is a reality that has such traits, and that this reality is supreme. However, anyone who thinks that value commitments are not rationally defensible is just as likely to be skeptical about this claim as well.

Another approach for the theist is to appeal to our raw intuitions in the following way. All other things being equal, with which kind of reality would it make sense to be more concerned about having a good relationship? All other things being equal, it would seem to make sense to be more concerned with a reality that is eternal, necessary, and independent, rather than one that is mortal, contingent, and dependent. If so, based on the pragmatic criterion mentioned earlier, it makes more sense to conceive of God as having the former features rather than the latter ones.

Still another approach for the theist is to claim it makes sense to think that certain features or properties are *objectively better* than others. In fact, many people (including many atheists) would agree that a being or reality that is necessary, eternal, and so on, is in some *objective* sense "superior" to one that is not. However, to articulate this point more fully, some account of "goodness" or "what makes a being or reality good" must be provided. The following account draws on a line of thought found in many classic sources in ancient and medieval philosophy, namely, one that aims to connect the notion of "goodness" with that of "being."[14]

As Aristotle pointed out, we often speak of things as "good" or "bad" *insofar as they fulfill some specific function.*[15] This is sometimes known as "instrumental good" or "instrumental value." For example, we can speak of a good orange, a good car, a good pianist (or even a good assassin) in terms of whether those things or beings fulfill a certain specific task. Precisely what is the proper task of any of these things may be difficult to formulate. It may even be a matter of debate as to what is the proper function of an orange or car, and it may even be arbitrary in some sense. (Suppose I happen to be interested in using an orange as a paperweight. In that case, what makes the orange "good" or "bad" differs drastically from what would normally make it "good.") But surely, the most important question to ask about something is whether it is good or bad *insofar as its being or reality is concerned.* This way of phrasing the question asks about the thing most fundamentally, and not merely about some particular function that the thing may or may not have. Thus, for example, although a given object may be a better *car* than a given human person, that does not make the car a better *being* than the human. Similarly, a given human person may be a better *pianist* (or *assassin*) than another, but that does not make him better *as a being*. Our question comes down to this: is there some rationally defensible way of determining what makes something "good" insofar as it is a being or reality – and not merely insofar as it fulfills some particular function which it may or may not assume?[16] Differently stated, is there some rationally defensible way of determining that something is *intrinsically* or *inherently* good, rather than merely *instrumentally* good?

Now, the theist may propose that it *does* make sense to say, at least in certain cases, that there are certain features which render one being or reality more significant or "metaphysically better" than another – precisely insofar as the two beings or realities are compared *as beings or realities*. In particular, it makes sense to say that that which is eternal, necessary, and independent is superior *in its very being or reality* (that is, *intrinsically* superior) to anything that is mortal, contingent, and dependent. A being that is mortal or contingent is in some sense defective in its very being. A being that is eternal and necessary lacks that particular defect.[17] Furthermore, it's not merely that the one being is "a lot better" in its being than the other.

Rather, the difference is one of kind, not degree. Hence, it makes sense to think that in this case, the superiority is *qualitative* rather than merely quantitative.

Furthermore, the theist may propose that it makes sense to think of that which has the power or capacity to be the causal source or explanatory ground of all else as qualitatively superior *in its very being or reality* to all else. Such a being or reality must have a certain "metaphysical richness", so to speak, which any other being or reality would lack. There must be something about the very nature or essence of that being or reality which enables it to be the causal source or ground of all else. Whatever that "metaphysical richness" is, and however it is to be understood or explained, it renders that being or reality metaphysically *qualitatively superior* to any other possible being or reality.[18]

This brief account provides some rationale for the theist to think that certain features or properties render one being or reality metaphysically qualitatively superior to all else. Nothing said here *identifies* or *reduces* the notion of goodness to the notion of reality or being. Moreover, nothing said here implies that it is possible to rank all possible things or beings on a scale of being or "goodness." Finally, there is no claim here that everybody is rationally compelled to think of an eternal, necessary, independent being that is the causal source of all other possible things as *qualitatively superior* to all else. However, many people, perhaps even many atheists and agnostics, would agree with that claim. Of course, even if one goes along with this claim, one might wonder whether having these metaphysical features renders a being or reality better in *other* ways. Does having these superior metaphysical features render God better in a *moral* sense than a being that doesn't have them? It seems one could easily imagine a being or reality that is necessary, eternal, and so on, yet which has no volition or intellect at all. In this case it would not even be a "person," much less, a moral agent. We shall return to this point shortly.

God's "Ontological Category"

Perhaps the most fundamental question one can ask about the idea of God concerns God's ontological category. To ask about the "appropriate ontological category" under which God should be classified is to ask, what *kind* of being or reality is God? This question raises many difficult and complex philosophical issues. However, any articulation of the concept of God must address this question.

In what follows, we will sketch two views on God's ontological category, which are (or attempt to be) adequate for religious theism. We shall refer to these as the "standard" view and the "alternative" view. This is not to deny that there may be other theistic options as well. As far as the project of this book goes, either the standard or the alternative view will suffice. The overall argument of this book does not depend on how one settles this issue.

(A comparison of the relative merits of these views is relegated to an appendix.) Nevertheless, some view regarding God's ontological status is required for the purpose of this book.

Both of the following views make a distinction between God's *essence* and God's *secondary attributes*. Very roughly, God's essence is who or what God is most fundamentally. When we talk about God's necessary or metaphysical features we are talking about God's essence. God's secondary attributes are non-necessary features of God. Alternatively, they may be construed as the ways in which that essence reveals itself or acts, in ways that it need not have. Additionally, both alternatives hold that there is some sense in which God is "ineffable", or indescribable, or mysterious.

The standard conception: God as a being; divine traits as properties

The first view is perhaps the more popular one among contemporary philosophers of religion.[19] We may label this the *standard conception* of God. On this view, God is conceived as *a being* or *a particular entity* – a very special being or entity of course, but *a being* nonetheless. God is conceived as a being that has the metaphysical properties mentioned above: necessity, independence, and so on. Additionally, God has certain secondary attributes (benevolence, compassion, justice, and so on) that somehow apply or pertain to God's essence. Typically, the secondary attributes are conceived as contingent properties or aspects of God. It is by virtue of the divine attributes (both necessary and contingent ones) that God has caused, and continues to sustain and manage the world. Or, as some might prefer to put it, talk about God's attributes (or, talk about at least *some* of those attributes) is to be construed as talk about the different ways in which God's essence acts or reveals itself.[20]

This conception takes God as the *causal source* of the universe. God is conceived as the being who has caused, and continues to sustain, the existence of all things in the universe. God himself has no external causal source. Either he is not in need of a cause, or he is uncaused, or self-caused, or continuously self-causing, or some such thing. Exactly what are the secondary divine attributes, the details of how they operate, and why those attributes are the way they are is a matter for separate discussion.

On the standard conception, many questions still remain for the theologian to address. Perhaps the main one concerns how best to understand God's necessity. What is it about God's being that makes it necessary that God exist? Is God somehow *logically* necessary? And, if God is not conceived as logically necessary, what kind of necessity does he have? Another set of issues concerns the divine attributes. How are the attributes related? Which attributes are necessary and which are secondary or contingent?[21] Why does God have the attributes he has, and not others? The theist may respond that those attributes that are necessary do not need an explanation or are somehow self-explanatory. But what about the secondary or contingent attributes? What explains them? How do the contingent attributes relate to the necessary ones? A full-fledged theology would have to address such questions. However, at some stage, the theologian may simply have to say that we cannot answer all these questions completely. There is a limit to how far we can articulate our understanding of the concept of God.

The alternative conception: God as Being; divine traits as principles

Let us turn now to a different approach on how to conceive of God's ontological category.[22] This approach also understands God as the "Supreme Person." However, this alternative conceives of God's essence not as *a being*, but rather as *Being*. Since this alternative seems less popular today than the standard conception, we shall refer to it as "the alternative conception."[23] This alternative takes the necessary attributes mentioned above (eternality, independence, and so on) not as properties that inhere in *a being*, nor as ways of talking about what that being lacks (as in negative theology), but rather as *features or aspects of Being*. In addition, this alternative conceives of God's *secondary attributes* (benevolence, compassion, justice) not as properties that inhere in some special being, nor as ways of talking about how that being acts, but rather as *principles* or *laws*, which describe the basic ways in which Being (that is, God on this conception) is exhibited or expressed in the world. To articulate all this, we must first try to clarify what is meant by the term, *Being*, as opposed to *a being*.

Consider the following sentence (labeled "R"):

R = Every stop sign exhibits or manifests *redness*.

There is no denying that in some sense this sentence is true. All red things have "redness" in common. A particular red thing such as a stop sign manifests or displays redness. Now the term "*redness*" here is not merely shorthand for talking about *every thing that is red*. For, R is not saying, "every stop sign exhibits *every thing that is red*" (though in some sense, perhaps that sentence is true). Second, the term "redness" does not name a particular, concrete entity.[24] The term "redness" is an abstract noun. Does that mean that "redness" is "purely mental" or "purely verbal"? This is a vexed philosophical question which we need not enter. No matter how one understands the ontological status of "redness," sentence R above is true.

Now consider the following sentence (labeled "E"):

E = Every being exhibits or manifests *being*.

Again, there is no denying that in some sense E is true. All beings have something in common, and that is being. Any particular being manifests or displays being. The question is, what does the term *being* here mean (in its *second* occurrence in E)? Again, the term "being" here does not mean "everything that exists" or the "totality of all things." For, E is not saying "every being that exists exhibits every being that exists" (though that sentence might be true in some sense). And again, the term "being" here need not be taken to refer to a *particular being*.[25] One might want to say, the term "being" here names a property. There is a philosophical dispute about whether it is correct to view existence or being as a property. Perhaps the safest thing to say is that the term "being" here is an abstract noun. This is just the way we used the term "redness" in the sentence "all stop signs manifest redness." We can leave open whether it is correct to view being as a property, or something which is purely mental or verbal.

To make clear when we intend to use the term "being" in the abstract sense we might use a term like *being-ness* or *being-hood*. Alternatively, instead of creating new words, we may simply capitalize the word "Being" when we intend to use it in the abstract sense as opposed to the concrete sense. Thus we may restate E as follows:

E = Every being exhibits or manifests Being.[26]

Having made the distinction between *Being* as opposed to *a being*, let us return to our discussion of God. The alternative conception of God's ontological status identifies the essence of God as Being in the sense just described.[27] On this view, God's essence is not a *being* at all. Hence, on this view, it would be incorrect to say, "God's essence exists" – for the only sort of thing than can exist (or fail to exist) is *a* being (or something which is conceived as *a being*). It is also incorrect to say "God's essence is true" since the only sort of thing that can be true (or false) is (something which is conceived as) a proposition or statement. On this alternative, the properties or predicates "exists" or "is true" simply do not apply to God's essence.[28]

On this approach, God's metaphysical attributes may be understood as follows. The basic idea is still the same: God's essence is conceived as primal, foundational, ultimate. After all, what could be more primal or ultimate than Being itself? Furthermore, when we reflect on Being, we notice that Being has certain features. On this conception, the aspects of *necessity, independence, eternality, uncreatedness* and *uniqueness* may be understood not as properties of a being (as the standard conception would have it) but rather as *necessary features of Being*.[29] This requires explanation.

God's *independence, uncreatedness* and *eternality* may be understood as follows. Being does not depend on something else for its being. It *is* being, that's just what it is. In this sense, Being, that is, God's essence, is independent. Furthermore, Being cannot become not-being. It never was not-being and it never will be the case that Being becomes non-being. This might sound confusing or sophistical at first. But it is no more confusing or sophistical than saying, for example, that necessarily, redness is not greenness, it never was greenness, and it never will be greenness. Of course, a red *thing* can become green. Similarly, perhaps, any thing that exists can pass out of existence. But being itself cannot ever be anything other than Being. Similarly, God's *necessity* may be understood as follows. Necessarily, Being is being. Using somewhat more old-fashioned language, we might say that it is of the very nature of Being that it is Being. This is much like saying, necessarily, redness is redness. It is not as if it just so happens, as a matter of empirical fact or circumstance, that Being is Being. Note that on this approach (unlike the standard conception) the theist is *not* committed to the notion that there is (or could be) *a particular being* that is independent, uncreated, eternal, and necessary.[30] Rather, these are features that pertain to Being.

On this view, God is not (and could not be) the causal source of all other things; at least not in the way this is standardly understood. For, on the present view, God is not an entity that causes and sustains other things. Rather, God's essence (Being) is conceived as the condition or ontological ground of all things. As we have already said, there is at least some sense in which it is true that all beings (including all contingent beings) exhibit Being. Similarly, God's *uniqueness* may be understood along the same lines. Being is unlike any other abstraction, such as redness, triangularity, and so on. Being is fundamental in a way that nothing else is. Redness is a color like other colors, triangularity is a shape like other shapes, and so on. Only some things that exist depend ontologically on redness or triangularity. But *all* things that exist depend on Being. Hence, Being is unique. Again, the claim here is not that all things depend *causally* on being. Rather the dependence here is a logical or ontological relationship.

At this stage, the reader might be inclined to object in the following way. The present account identifies God's essence with Being in the abstract sense. We have also argued that it is in some sense obviously true that "all beings exhibit Being." Suppose one agrees with everything that has been said so far. Doesn't this conception simply define "God" in such a way that the only way to be an atheist is to reject E above? This seems absurd; everyone who accepts E will turn out to be a theist! And surely, there's more to theism than simply the belief that "every being exhibits Being"! Furthermore, isn't that assertion philosophically trivial? How can any religious theist possibly think of God as an *abstraction*, and be willing to leave open the possibility that God's essence is purely mental or verbal? Isn't this tantamount to asserting that God is "just an idea"?

These objections might be valid if all there was to theism on the alternative conception is what has been said so far. But, there is more to theism on this alternative; indeed a lot more. So far we have been discussing only the notion of God's *essence* on this alternative. But this alternative also proposes a certain conception of the divine *secondary attributes* as well. On the present alternative, this is where the real difference between theism and atheism really lies.

On this alternative, the theist understands the divine secondary attributes (benevolence, compassion, justice, and so on) as *principles* that govern the existence and operations of the world. By a "principle" is meant a general law, which describes some fundamental truth about how the universe operates.[31] It is these principles that, according to the theist, describe the basic ways in which Being (God's essence) is exhibited in the world. Differently stated, the principles describe *the structure of the manifestation of Being*. So, while it may indeed be philosophically trivial to say "every being exhibits Being," it will not be trivial to make specific assertions about the basic ways in which that manifestation or exhibition is structured.[32] It is here where the atheist and the theist part company.

What does it mean to say that God's secondary attributes are to be understood as principles? We may articulate this as follows. As human beings, we seek to explain things, events, and so on in terms of principles or laws. When we ask what is the explanation of those principles, we seek to find other more general or more universal principles. The object of science is to formulate certain very general or universal laws or principles that are empirically discoverable and testable, using certain methodologies (quantitative methods; repeatable laboratory tests, and so on). Some scientists are working on the question of whether there is a way of uniting all the various scientific laws under one general theory. Now, the theist's notion is that there are certain divine principles that underlie the scientific principles (and that may not be knowable using scientific methodologies). For, even supposing one could formulate all the scientific laws, one could still ask, *why* are the scientific laws the way they are? The theist's notion is that beyond the scientific laws lies a deeper explanation: there are certain *divine principles* (benevolence, compassion, justice, and so on) in light of which the scientific laws and the initial conditions are (or were) the way they are (or were). In other words, according to the theist, the world is the way it is because it fits into a certain divine scheme or structure. The "divine principles" are ways of talking about that structure.[33]

As was the case with the standard conception, the second alternative still leaves many unanswered questions. Perhaps the main one is, *why* are the principles the way they are, rather than some other way? Differently stated, *why* is it that Being is manifested or exhibited in certain ways rather than others? Notice how this question parallels one of the questions remaining on the standard conception mentioned above, namely, why are divine secondary attributes the way they are rather than some other way? A full-fledged theology would have to address such questions. Yet, at some stage, the theologian may have to insist there is a limit to how far we can answer such questions.

In the Appendix we shall consider some of the relative strengths and weaknesses of these two conceptions of God's ontological status. But perhaps the main motivation for why many theists tend to prefer the standard conception to the alternative concerns the following. All theists conceive of God as a *person*. And, to many theists it seems that one may conceive of God as a person only if one conceives of God as a *being*. Now, if God's essence is identified as Being, and God's secondary attributes are constituted by a set of principles, doesn't that automatically render God "impersonal"? How can one conceive of God as a set of principles and still view God as caring, choosing, loving, and so on? The next subsection seeks to show, among other things, that the ascription of personhood to God is compatible with the conception of God's essence as Being.

God's Volitional and Intellectual Superiority (Divine Personhood)

The religious theist conceives of God not only as metaphysically supreme, but also as a *person*. God is not merely the cause or ground for all that is, but rather, God is a *certain kind* of cause or ground. Roughly speaking, the term "person" connotes that God is a rational, free agent. In other words, God is capable of intelligent and willful action. It is by virtue of his personhood that God is capable of communicating with other persons, and capable of adopting certain cognitive attitudes such as love and respect toward other persons, including humans. It is by virtue of his personhood that it is possible for God to enter and sustain "interpersonal relationships" with other persons, including those of mutual recognition and love. Furthermore, God is not just a person; God is the *Supreme* Person. We shall take this to mean that God's intelligence and freedom are *qualitatively superior* to the intelligence and freedom of other beings (such as humans).

Our main concern here is to articulate what it means for God to be a Supreme Person in a way that is compatible with God's metaphysical supremacy. Our second concern will be to discuss what motivation or rationale the religious theist has for thinking that a being or reality that is supreme would not only have the metaphysical features already described, but also have personhood.

Earlier we considered two ways of understanding God's ontological status. We must articulate the notion of God as a person both on the standard and alternative conceptions of God. On the standard conception of God as a being, the account of God's personhood goes something like this. To qualify as a person, a being must be *rational* and *free*.

Basically, a being is *rational* if it can know and think about the world. To say, for example, that "God knows that John has committed murder" is to say that the being, God, is aware of that event, and will act in a certain way given his other attributes. God has "intentional states." God knows the world, and God utilizes that information in deciding what to do and what events to cause. Generally, theists think of God as "omniscient" that is, knowing all truths.[34] God is aware of everything that goes on in the world, and he uses that information in order to make his choices.

The other crucial aspect involved in personhood is that God is *free*. On the standard conception, a being is *free* if it can knowingly cause certain events to take place in a way that is neither random, nor constrained by any force.[35] Differently stated, a being "acts freely" only if it causes events *for a reason*, and only if it is not constrained to act by anything. We need to add the phrase, *for a reason* because a free action is not the same thing as a random, inexplicable or "uncaused" event. Only a free being can plot actions and intelligently communicate with other beings. Only a free being can genuinely be said to "interact" with other persons in the world. A free being "interacts" with others only if it chooses to do certain things based partly on consideration of what other events have occurred, some of which may be the result of the free actions of other persons.

On this conception, God is a being who thinks, knows, plans and deliberates about what to do in the world. God acts and reacts to the world based partly on how other free persons act. Exactly what God chooses (or has chosen) to do is another matter. Needless to say, different theistic religions disagree about what God (if he exists) has done, or about how God acts in general. In any case, God is depicted as a being that *speaks* to humans and also *responds* to human speech, at least on some occasions. On the standard conception, God "speaks" to prophets when God causes certain words to be heard by the prophet, whereby God intends to communicate a certain message. God "responds" to prayer when God understands what human persons are asking for and then causes certain events to take place that fulfill those prayers.[36]

One might be inclined to ask, what does it really mean for a metaphysically supreme being to "think and know about the world"? Does God act and react to our actions by understanding what we do and then deciding to act in a certain manner? Does God deliberate and plot out courses of action? Does God know about the world by "inspecting" it somehow, the way humans find out about the world? Does he make decisions after "weighing alternatives" and seeing how things work out in practice? Surely, God's way of knowing the world must be rather different than ours, since, typically, God is conceived in such a way that he does not have a body, and so he does not have sense organs which process information in the way that humans do.

Assuming one could answer these questions, there still remains the question of *why* God makes the choices he does. Why, for example, has God chosen to cause or create the world? Perhaps the theist does not *need* to have an answer to this question in order for the conception of God to be coherent. Nevertheless, one traditional way of answering this last question is to say that God's creation is a form of his own self-expression.[37] In other words, God's free action is in some sense *a free expression of his own necessary nature*. God's choice to create the world is a contingent event, but it is through that choice that God's necessary nature is made manifest. On this approach, the divine secondary attributes are in some sense explicable by appeal to God's necessary properties. The theist might also suggest that the specific ways in which God expresses himself make sense, given the specific necessary features that God has. Later on, we shall have some comment on how this suggestion might be developed (see the discussion of God's moral character below).

Now let us turn to the alternative conception described above, where God is not conceived as *a being* but rather as Being. On the alternative conception, one may take the ascription of rationality or knowledge to God not as an ascription of a mental state to a being, but rather as a way of talking about the fundamental order or structure of the universe. To say, for example, that "God knows that John has committed murder" is to say that there is a certain divine scheme or structure that is operative in the world, and that, in light of that divine scheme, the fact that John has committed murder will have certain consequences rather than others. Precisely what those consequences will be depends on other divine principles (such as benevolence and justice; more on those principles below). Generalizing this point, for God *to know all true facts*[38] means roughly that there is a divine scheme at work in the world, such that in light of all true facts, certain things will happen rather than others. Any true fact may, if relevant, play some explanatory role in what happens later, given the divine principles in accord with which the world exists and operates.

How might we understand God's freedom on the alternative conception? Instead of saying that God is a being who *causes* things to happen, we may say that there is a set of fundamental or divine principles, which *explain* why things happen. Instead of saying that God is a being who is not constrained to act by any circumstances, we may say that the divine principles are the ultimate set of principles for which there is no further set of principles in terms of which those principles can be explained.[39] Instead of saying that God is the being who, by virtue of his wisdom, designed the cosmos and the operations of nature in a structured and orderly way, we may say that the structure and order of the world is to be explained by the fact that it fits into a divine scheme or plan which is itself orderly. Finally, instead of saying that God is a being who interacts with persons in the world by causing things to happen in the world depending partly on how we act, we may say that the world is organized in accord with certain divine principles (for example, benevolence, justice) in just such a way that, based partly on how we act, certain events occur (for example, reward or punishment for those actions).[40]

How will this alternative approach understand the notion of *divine communication*? Instead of saying that the phrase "God speaks" means that the being, God, causes certain auditory experiences in the ear or mind of the prophet, one would say that certain auditory events occur in the prophet's ear (or consciousness) that are to be explained by appeal to the divine principles and by the fact that those auditory events fit into the divine plan as described by those principles. And, instead of saying that the phrase "God responds to prayer" means that the being, God, understands human prayers and on occasion chooses to answer them, one would say that, given the divine principles which describe the underlying structure and operations of the world, there are some occasions when prayers result in a positive response.

Some religious theists may feel that something crucial about God's personhood is lost on this alternative conception. However, it seems there is no pragmatic difference between the two views. That is, there is no difference from the point of view of the phenomena, so to speak, on the human end. On either view, righteous actions are rewarded and evil actions are punished. The degree to which God is "involved" in the world is (or could be) exactly the same as well. How intimately God "cares" about what people do – or how "fine grained" the divine principles are – is an open question on either the standard or alternative conception. (More on the issue of divine providence follows below.)

On the alternative account, as on the standard conception, certain questions still remain unanswered. For example, *why* are the divine principles true? *Why* are the divine principles the way they are rather than some other way? Why is it, for example, that there is an orderly divine plan at work? The theist may suggest that the secondary divine principles are in some sense explicable by appeal to the necessary features of God.[41] How this might work in detail is a matter upon which we shall have some comment later (see discussion of God's moral character below). In summary so far, whether God's attributes are conceived as properties that inhere in a being, or as divine principles that describe the manifestation or expression of Being in the world, the theist can give an equally coherent account of what it means to ascribe personhood to God.

Regardless of whether one adopts the standard or alternative conception of God's ontological status, another rather different objection against the notion of God as a person concerns the issue of *immutability*. Some (for example, some ancient Greek philosophers and some non-theistic Hindus) would argue that "metaphysical supremacy" *requires* a kind of immutability, which is incompatible with personhood.[42] The argument has been made that whereas any person is subject to fundamental or essential change, a metaphysically supreme reality would *not* be subject to such change. The theist might respond in several ways. One response is simply to admit that the theist does not conceive of God as immutable. Another response is to make a distinction between different kinds of change: essential change and non-essential change. One can say that God himself, conceived either in the standard way as a being, or on the alternative way as Being itself, does not undergo *essential* change. Nor do his properties or features change, either. Rather, on the standard conception, one would say that his *actions* change, or what he *causes* change. On the alternative conception, it is only the events in the world which change, despite the fact that those events are explicable by appeal to divine principles that do not change. Thus in effect, despite the fact that God has volition, God does not change essentially at all.[43]

Thus far we have argued that ascription of personhood to God is *compatible* with his metaphysical supremacy, whether God is conceived as a being, or as Being. We need next to say something about what it means for God to have *supreme* personhood. One traditional way of understanding this would be to conceive of God as omniscient ("all knowing") and omnipotent ("all powerful"). However, all the theist needs to say is that God's knowledge and power is *qualitatively superior* to that of any other possible kind of thing. God's knowledge and power is of a different order than anything else's; that does not obviously entail that he knows all truths that are logically possible to know.[44] For the present purpose, the theist need only say the following. Since God is not dependent on any being or reality external to himself, divine freedom is the best kind of freedom. It is not that God has *quantitatively* more freedom than anything else. Anything else that exists will depend for its freedom (if it has any at all) upon God and his properties (or upon the principles which describe the structure and operations of the world). In this way, there is a *qualitative* difference between God's freedom and the freedom of anything else. In this sense, God is the supreme person. The kind of freedom God has is unique.

Our next concern is whether there is some way of rationally motivating the notion that a supreme reality or being would be a person or have personhood. First, it is open for the theist to assert flatly that God's metaphysical supremacy is logically independent from his intellectual and volitional supremacy. He might, for example, hold that we have learned through religious experience or revelation that the supreme reality has personhood. However, it would seem strange if the two (God's metaphysical supremacy and God's personhood) are not somehow integrally related – as if it *just so happened* to be the case that God is both metaphysically supreme and also a person. The theist's conception of God is more conceptually plausible if there is some reason for thinking that a supreme reality is also one that has personhood.

The notion that persons are intrinsically superior to non-persons is not only a traditional theistic teaching about God. It is an important biblical doctrine that is expressed in the teaching that man is made in the divine image. It is also manifested in the biblical teachings regarding respect for other human persons; there is something sacred about persons compared to beasts, plants, and other creatures. This view has important ramifications for the theist's conception of the good relationship with God, and consequently for the conception of how one goes about pursuing that relationship.[45] Therefore it behooves the theist to motivate the position that there is something special about persons (aside possibly from relying on revelation). What's so special about personhood? Is there a rationale for this or is it just a blind preference of some sort?

One way to argue for this is to use an "intuition pump" approach as follows. Ask yourself this question: which would you rather be, a person or a non-person? Would you rather be a being or reality capable of making choices or not? Would you rather be a being or reality capable of entering and sustaining mutual relationships of recognition and love, or not? Many people will answer yes. If they do, that means they think that personhood is better than non-personhood. Furthermore, one may pose the issue pragmatically. Namely, which way of looking at God offers potentially greater value for the relationship with God? If God lacks personhood, he lacks *responsibility*. Which is potentially better – a relationship with a responsible being or one that lacks responsibility? Furthermore, if God lacks responsibility, he is not capable of moral behavior, much less, moral supremacy. If the relationship with God is going to have any moral dimension at all, God must be conceived as a person.

However, it could be argued that all this just reflects a bias on our part to favor persons. As mentioned earlier, some philosophers (certain ancient Greek and Hindu thinkers) insist that indeed it is better for God or the ultimate reality to be conceived as *non*-personal. For some of these thinkers, it is better to be a non-person than a person. In fact, for some of these thinkers, the goal of religion is to emulate and/or merge with the impersonal reality and indeed lose one's own personality in the process. Can the theist provide some rationally defensible way to support the judgment that it is better to be a person than not?

One way to argue for this is by extending the argument given earlier. We had argued that the most important question to ask about something is whether it is good or bad *qua* being or reality; in other words, *qua* "what it is" most fundamentally. We suggested that it *makes sense* to regard a reality that is necessary, eternal, and independent as metaphysically superior (superior in its very being) to one that is contingent, mortal, and dependent. We also suggested it makes sense to think that that which is the causal source or ontological ground of all else is metaphysically superior to that which is not the source or ground. Our reasoning was that if some being or reality is (or could be) the cause or ground of all else, it must contain within itself a certain "metaphysical richness," so to speak, which any other being or reality would lack. No matter how that "metaphysical richness" is understood, there must be something about the very nature or essence of that being or reality which enables it to be the causal source or ground of all else.

Now the same line of argument can be extended to argue that such a being or reality is even *more* superior if it is free. There are (at least) two ways x can be the cause or ground of y. It could be that x is a *free* cause or ground of y or that x is *not* a free cause or ground of y. But which kind of cause or ground is metaphysically superior? If it is not a free cause or ground, then, it was constrained to do whatever it has done by circumstances beyond its control. If it was so constrained, x really doesn't contain within itself the wherewithal to cause or ground y.[46] Hence, a *free* cause or ground is superior to one that is not free. It follows that a *supreme* reality or being should be conceived of as the *free* cause or ground of all else. And, since only persons are free, it follows that the supreme reality or being should be conceived as a person.[47]

More generally, the theist's position is that any free being or reality is inherently superior (as a reality or being) to a non-free one. A being or reality that has the wherewithal to cause or ground something else is metaphysically superior to one that does not. But, any being that is not free cannot be the genuine cause or ground of anything else. It can only do what it is constrained to do. The ability to cause or ground something else is a metaphysically better attribute only if that ability is free.

Incidentally, the argument given here would apply not only to God but more broadly as well. We have offered a rationale for thinking that, in general, having freedom makes a being more superior than it would be otherwise. Thus, humans (assuming they have freedom) are superior to both animals and plants (assuming the latter lack freedom). Freedom is qualitatively a different power than brute strength. Thus, a frail person (if he has freedom) is more intrinsically valuable than a mighty beast (assuming it lacks freedom).[48] This might be one reason why we place such a high premium on free choice or autonomy.[49] However, the issue of what kind of freedom humans have (or animals lack) is beyond the scope of this book.

In any case, if indeed freedom makes for a metaphysically better being or reality, then, the better the freedom, the better the being. Hence, a supreme reality would not only have freedom; it would have the best *kind* of freedom. Moreover, given the notion of God as necessary, uncreated, independent, and eternal, and the notion of God as the free cause or ground of all things, it stands to reason that God's intelligence and freedom would be qualitatively superior to those found in contingent, created, dependent, and mortal beings. It is qualitatively superior in just the sense described above: the freedom of dependent creatures is derivative from God himself; divine freedom is not derivative at all.

In summary, we have argued that the ascription of personhood to God *coheres* with the notion of God as metaphysically supreme. This holds whether or not one conceives of God's essence as a being or as Being. Second, we have articulated what motivates the religious theist to think of the supreme reality or being as having supreme personhood. But even if God is a person, that still leaves open what kind of person God is. This brings us to the next topic.

God's Moral or "Character" Superiority (Divine Personality)

So far we have said that God is metaphysically supreme, and that God's personhood is supreme, that is, his intelligence and freedom are qualitatively superior to any other possible reality. But even this does not go far enough as a description of the concept of God. One could imagine a being or reality that is metaphysically supreme, and that has great intelligence and freedom, but which does not act morally at all. For the religious theist, God not only acts morally; God is in some sense "morally supreme." God is conceived as having certain especially good character traits; for example, benevolence, compassion, and justice. We shall reserve the term God's "personhood" to refer to God's agency (the notion that God is rational and free) and use the term God's "personality" to refer to God's character traits (the specific or characteristic way or ways in which God uses his freedom).

For the religious theist, just as God's personhood is conceived as qualitatively superior, so too God's personality is conceived as qualitatively superior. God is not merely "more benevolent" and "more just" than anything else; rather, God's benevolence and justice are qualitatively *superior* to that of anyone else.[50] Precisely what these traits amount to, and in what way God has these traits in a qualitatively superior way, is a matter of interpretation and debate among theologians and philosophers of religion.

Here arises a set of issues similar to those discussed above regarding the relation between God's metaphysical supremacy and God's personhood. Our first concern will be to defend the view that the conception of God as morally supreme is not incompatible with God's other features or properties, that is, God's metaphysical, intellectual, and volitional supremacy. Our second concern will be to discuss what motivation the religious theist can offer for supposing that a reality which is metaphysically, intellectually and volitionally supreme would also be one that is *morally* supreme.

Before proceeding, it is worth emphasizing that here we have adopted the view that God's moral character is *contingent*. Differently stated, God's benevolence and justice are not necessary features of God; they are "secondary attributes." The idea of God as morally supreme is the idea of a God that *unfailingly but freely* chooses the right thing (or the thing that is as right as can possibly be under the circumstances). It is not a matter of luck that God is benevolent; nor is it necessary that God be benevolent. We may follow our earlier suggestion on how to explicate the notion of divine freedom. We had suggested that God's secondary attributes are to be explained, but not necessitated, by God's necessary features or properties. So the theist may regard God's moral character as explained, but not necessitated, by God's necessary nature. We shall return to this point later.

We have already claimed it is coherent to think of God both as metaphysically supreme and as having supreme personhood. If what we have said so far is correct, then, there does not seem to be any logical incoherency in the ascription of a moral character – indeed, a *supreme* moral character – to God. To show that it is coherent, all we can do is articulate further what it means to say that God has a supreme moral character. We need to do this for the standard conception of God as a being, and for the alternative conception of God as Being.

On the standard conception, God is a being who freely chooses how to act. The secondary attributes are conceived as contingent properties of that being. If so, it is, so to speak, "up to God" to choose how he acts. There seems to be no *a priori* reason to think that God could not choose to act morally, under any and all possible circumstances. To say that *God is benevolent* is to say roughly that, as a matter of course, God causes undeserved good things to happen. To say that *God is just* is to say roughly that God rewards the righteous and punishes the wicked. Perhaps more fundamentally, it is to say that God has created a world in which humans are given the option of being righteous or wicked, and that subsequently, God rewards the righteous and punishes the wicked. That is, God creates a world in which there are free, responsible agents who can achieve merit (or demerit). Furthermore, given his metaphysical, intellectual, and volitional supremacy, it seems there is nothing to prevent God from behaving in a way that is maximally benevolent and maximally just. That is, he is as benevolent and just as he can possibly be. On every occasion wherever possible, God causes the most benevolent act that is consistent with God's unfailing concern for justice.[51] Finally, there may be other moral attributes as well, such as compassion. A full theology would attempt to describe all of these attributes.

On the alternative conception, God is conceived as Being, and the secondary attributes are conceived as contingent principles in accord with which the world operates. All talk of God's personality traits are understood as ways of talking about the fundamental order or structure of the world, that is to say, about the kinds of things that happen in the universe. For example, to say "God is benevolent" would mean that there is a certain principle operative in the world, such that *undeserved good things happen*. Similarly to say that "God is just" means roughly that *the world is organized in such a way that righteousness and wickedness are genuine options for human beings*, and that, over the course of time, *the righteous are rewarded and the wicked are punished for their deeds*. There seems to be nothing logically incoherent in the scenario just described. Furthermore there seems to be nothing incoherent in supposing that these principles are maximally operative, that is, they operate mutually in the best way that is logically possible. Precisely what all that amounts to in detail may be difficult to describe. And, again, there may be other moral principles as well, such as divine compassion.

On either the standard or alternative view, maximal benevolence and justice seem reducible to the notion that God *always* does what is morally best (if such an action is available). If that were the whole story, it would seem that God's moral superiority to others is only a quantitative, not a qualitative matter. However, aside from the maximal nature of God's benevolence and justice, there is another dimension to God's moral supremacy implicit in what has already been said. Since God is metaphysically, intellectually, and volitionally supreme, it follows that God has what we might call *supreme responsibility*. It is widely accepted that a being or reality has the capacity for genuine moral activity (and is thereby genuinely worthy of moral praise and blame) only insofar as it is *free*. As articulated earlier, God's freedom is radically superior to that of dependent creatures. So, whereas the moral activity of any dependent being is not free in the fullest sense, God's moral activity is as free as can possibly be. A similar point may be made in connection with God's intelligence or rationality. Moral decisions made by human persons are made under conditions of partial knowledge and sometimes under false information. But, since God is intellectually supreme, all the relevant facts (or at least, all the relevant facts that it is logically possible for some being or reality to know) are always taken into account.[52] For these reasons, God is conceived as radically *responsible* for his actions. His responsibility is qualitatively superior to that of any other possible person. Therefore, if and when he chooses to act morally, he is radically more *praiseworthy* for doing so than any human can ever be. So, if it is logically coherent to think of God as maximally benevolent and just, it is logically coherent to think of God not only as morally better than any other possible kind of thing, but also as morally supreme in a qualitative sense.

One potential objection is worth mentioning.[53] Earlier we considered and responded to the objection that a supreme reality should not be conceived as personal on the grounds that a supreme reality would not be mutable. With regard to the notion of God as moral, here a different but related objection arises. Some critics of theism might object that even if it were allowed that a supreme reality may be mutable (subject to change) in some sense, it still should not be conceived as *passible* (subject to being affected by external events beyond its control). Yet, if God is morally supreme, he must be "compassionate." If so, it seems God is not only mutable but also passible, for compassion involves the ability to be affected by events that are external to oneself, such as the suffering of others.

However, again the theist may respond by distinguishing between essential and non-essential change. The theist may insist that God does not essentially change. Nor do his properties change; only his acts change. God is essentially not passible, but his actions are such that what he does depends on what people do. On the alternative conception, one may say that Being and the divine principles are *not* passible; rather that what happens in the world happens not only in accord with the principles but also depends on how people act. If the objector insists that in this case, God is not "really" compassionate, the theist could simply concede that God is not compassionate in the same way that humans are.

We have claimed that is coherent to think of God as metaphysically, intellectually, and volitionally supreme, as well as morally supreme. Still, this leaves open the question, what reason or motive is there in the first place to think that a being that is metaphysically, intellectually, and volitionally supreme would *also* be morally supreme? Again, there are several options for the theist here. The theist could simply assert that such is his conception of God. Or he could assert that he knows about God's personality based on religious experience or revelation. Another route here is to resort to the "intuition pump." What sounds better, a relationship with a supremely moral being, or with one that is less than supremely moral? It seems that a God who is morally supreme is potentially more worth our concern than one that isn't morally supreme.

However, the theist may attempt something more substantial here. We have already suggested why it makes sense to think of a supreme being as *free*. But if God is free, what kind of choices would God make? His choices could not be wholly random ones, nor could they be totally necessitated either. The only reasonable option seems to be that God would choose to do things that somehow *express his own nature*.[54] In other words, God would freely or *contingently* do things that in some way express or exhibit his essence and/or his *necessary* features. Putting the same point in terms of the alternative conception, the suggestion is that although the divine principles are contingently true, they are explicable in terms of the necessary features of Being. This may sound a bit paradoxical at first. In what follows, we shall describe how God's moral traits (benevolence and justice) may be viewed as ways in which God freely expresses his metaphysically supreme essence. In effect, this will provide a rationale for thinking that a metaphysically supreme being would also be a moral one. Such an account can be given, on both the standard and alternative conceptions of God.

On the standard conception, to say that God is benevolent is to say that God is the kind of being who causes undeserved good things. Typically, creation itself, the fostering and nourishing of all things are thought of as examples of divine benevolence. Now, we may easily view divine benevolence as a way in which God expresses his own essence.[55] By causing or creating contingent being, God is, in a sense, expressing his own nature as a being. Granted, contingent being is different from and metaphysically inferior to God's necessary being; but it is still being nonetheless. Thus the primary "benevolent" act is that of creation. Furthermore, God is eternal and everlasting. By continuously sustaining the world in existence, God continues to express or manifest himself as the eternal being. Granted, continuously sustained dependent existence is not the same thing as eternality. Still, this mimics or imitates God's eternal being. Thus, assuming that God acts in order to express himself, it makes sense that God would be "benevolent."

Furthermore, we claimed earlier that there is a rationally defensible way to make judgments about how "good" a being or reality is by considering its metaphysical properties, and/or by considering its "rank" in the order of being and power. We said that in a certain sense, creatures with freedom are better than creatures without freedom. Thus it makes sense to say that if God were to express his own supreme nature to the greatest extent possible, he would create not merely any world, but a world in which there are living things, and in which there are free creatures. This too falls under "benevolence." In this way, benevolence can be understood as a character trait which God possesses, whereby God expresses himself as the Supreme Being.

Now let us consider divine justice. Justice is the trait by which God rewards or punishes us based on our actions. In addition, justice is the trait whereby God gives us the opportunity to *merit* or *deserve* certain things. Divine justice may be viewed as an expression of divine *necessity* in the following way.[56] To say that God is necessary is to say that there is something about God's being *which makes it be what it is*. God's being is not a fluke or an accident; it *had* to be. There is a certain sense of "fixity" that pertains to God. God is what he is, not something other than that. Now, how might God express this aspect of himself, if at all? No matter what he does, God cannot create beings that are necessary in just the same way he is. However, there is something he can do which will allow dependent creatures to mimic or imitate divine necessity. This is to create beings (or at least some beings) in such a way that they can *justify* their own existence and their own rank in the order of things. They can do this if they can *earn* or *merit* their own status as beings. Thus, the attribute of divine justice can be viewed as an expression of God's necessity.

A parallel account can be given on the alternative conception, where God's essence is conceived not as *a being* but as Being. Given that the divine principles are ways in which Being is made manifest or exhibited, it makes sense to think that one of those principles would be the principle of benevolence. Divine benevolence is the principle that *undeserved good things happen* (such as, the coming into existence of the world, the flourishing of life, and so on). This principle may be explained by appeal to God's *Being* in the following way. At least one way (if not the primary way) in which Being is exhibited or made manifest is through the existence of contingent things, the flourishing of life. Similarly, divine justice may be explained by appeal to God's *necessity*. Divine justice is that *righteousness and wickedness are genuine options for human beings,* and that *the righteous are rewarded and the wicked punished*. Through the process of divine justice, the world better expresses a certain feature of God, namely his necessity. A world of creatures that exist, flourish, and grow wholly in accord with God's benevolence and without any merit or desert is a world that expresses God's essence in a deficient manner. Hence, an explanation for the principle of divine justice is attained by appealing to one of the features of Being, namely, necessity.

In summary so far, if we assume that God is metaphysically supreme and also free, it makes sense to think of God as benevolent and just as well. Another aspect of divine personality as traditionally conceived by many religious theists is that God is not only moral, but also "personal" in the sense that he is, or at least can be, intimately involved with human beings. This is sometimes referred to as the doctrine of "particular providence." We have argued that it makes sense to conceive of God as metaphysically, intellectually, volitionally, and morally supreme. If it makes sense to think of God as supremely moral, it stands to reason that indeed God would be intimately involved with his creatures, or at least, as intimately involved as one could reasonably expect a supreme person to be. No issue of any real moral weight would be too petty for a supreme person to be concerned with. Of course, the precise manner in which God is involved in the affairs of the world is another issue.[57] Theologians who accept particular providence may disagree over *how* particular that providence is to be conceived.

Another important point is that on the theistic conception of God, there is a high *a priori* probability that God will reveal himself, communicate his intentions, and seek to establish a relationship with the world. Though it is not *necessary* that he do so, his nature is such that we would reasonably expect him to do so, if he exists or is real. This is a point that we will return to later.

It is the task of philosophical theology to work out further details of the conception of God in a coherent way. There is no reason in principle to think that there aren't many different yet internally coherent ways of filling in those details. Needless to say, there is no guarantee that *every* way of filling in those details is coherent. The "tighter the fit" in one's concept of God, the better. If one thinks God has certain features, then, unless they are supported by empirical evidence, one would want those features not only to cohere, but also to be linked. (Perhaps this is just a desideratum of concepts generally.) It seems fair to say that the *more well developed* one's conception of God is without contradiction or inconsistency, the *more conceptually plausible* it becomes, and therefore the *more rationally defensible* it is for a person to have that conception. In any case, until and unless it can be shown otherwise, it is rationally defensible to conceive of God as the Supreme Person, in the ways described above.

It's worth noting that different religions tend to emphasize different aspects of the above mentioned features or properties of God. Even within the same religion, some theologians tend to emphasize different aspects of God. Some will claim that the metaphysical nature of God is most important. Some will claim that the intellectual aspect of God is foremost. Still others will claim that the moral aspects of God are more crucial than the other aspects. Even within the moral sphere, some will claim that certain moral features of God are more important than others (for example, compassion vs. justice). The variations on the concept of God that one finds among actual religions can be viewed as stemming from different ways of elaborating or organizing what's been set forth here. (If one starts with the notion that man is created in the image of God, then, indeed, these variations also go hand in hand with different views about human nature.) We need not enter into such issues. But, these views will have significant implications for the conception of the good relationship with God and the religious way.

Given that the religious theist has a certain conception of God, what does this entail about his commitments regarding the conceptual plausibility of *other* conceptions of God? And, what does this entail about his commitments regarding the plausibility of *non-theistic* conceptual frameworks? Needless to say, he will think that *some* other conceptions of God and *some* non-theistic frameworks contain aspects that are *incompatible* with his own conception. And, no doubt, he will be inclined to think that *some* other competing conceptions of God and some non-theistic frameworks *are* themselves internally incoherent. But he is not committed to thinking that *all* other competing conceptions are internally incoherent.

In fact, a religious theist could readily admit that there are other conceptions of God and that there are non-theistic frameworks that are a lot simpler and less paradoxical than his own theistic one. For example, a Christian might readily admit that his conception of the triune nature of God is somewhat more mysterious than that of, say, traditional Judaism, but so long as that conception is not logically contradictory, his conception may be rationally defensible. All that is necessary is that his own framework contains no logical contradiction. If this condition is met, then it is rationally defensible for him to have his conception of God, regardless of whether there are (or whether he thinks there are) alternative or competing frameworks that are also internally plausible. However, if he thinks that some other notion of God is *more* conceptually plausible than his own, one will begin to wonder why he holds fast to his conception. We shall return to this issue later.

3.3 The Conception of the Good Relationship with God

Next, we must address the conception of the good relationship with God. Our task is to articulate this idea and consider whether it is rationally defensible for a person to conceive of this relationship in such a way that it is supremely valuable. This is the way many religious theists conceive of that relationship, and, it is this kind of conception that is required for the argument of this book. Again, we cannot *prove* that this notion is conceptually plausible. All we can do is articulate the idea in a way that seems coherent, and address criticisms as they arise. We shall leave open how to fill in the details of this concept. Surely, *some* ways of conceiving of this relationship *are* incoherent. Also, *some* ways of conceiving of this relationship conflict with *some* ways of conceiving of God. One's conception of the good relationship with God should cohere with one's conception of God, as well as one's conception of the religious way.

There are at least three different ways one might conceive of the good relationship with God: 1) union with God, 2) obtaining some great good that is caused or explained by God, and 3) establishing an "interpersonal bond" with God. These three different ways of conceiving of that relationship "cut across" the two different ontological views about God described earlier. No matter which of those views one has about God's ontological status, there are still (at least) three versions of the good relationship with God. It seems also that one might put all three together into a combined view. But any defense mounted for thinking that such a combination is coherent will presumably rely on arguments for thinking that each one individually is coherent. Let us set aside the combined view, and consider each alternative separately.

Conception 1: Union with God

This conception takes the good relationship with God to be a "union" with God. We may distinguish two forms of this view. One is the *radical* view and one is the *moderate* view. The radical view is the notion that the religious person can somehow become *identical* with God.[58] This tends to be a view espoused by certain mystics. A more moderate view would be that while *identity* with God is impossible, one can gain some other type of intimate bond with God, so much so that somehow one partakes or shares in the divine nature, though without becoming *identical* to God. Exactly how that might work is itself no easy matter. But this latter position is not the radical view. In the present subsection, we are concerned only with the notion of union with God in its radical sense, where union with God means *identity* with God. We may treat the moderate view of union as a version of Conception 3 (see below).

The radical position sounds appealing at first blush, for it says that the good relationship with God consists in being identical with God himself. And what could be better than that? Surely, if it were possible at all, it would be better than any other possible condition for a human to attain. In that condition, one would just *be* God himself, the Supreme Person!

Unfortunately, this conception of the good relationship with God is logically incoherent. Regardless of how God's ontological status is understood, nothing can "become identical" with God. If two beings or realities are distinct at any point in time, then they cannot become identical at any later time. For it seems correct to assume that any two identical objects have precisely the same properties possessed by both objects at any time in the past or future (otherwise, they are not identical after all). One might try to understand the concept of "identity" here in a different sense, namely, where "becoming identical" with does not include gaining *all* the properties of the other object, but only those properties that do not make reference to the past. However, it would seem that, for example, God's necessity is not a feature that makes reference merely to the past. To say that a thing is necessary now is to say something about its present characteristics. Yet it would seem that nothing which is contingent to begin with, could *become* necessary at a later date, if and when it achieves the purported "union" with God. Thus the relationship in question seems incoherent or logically impossible. Nothing can "become identical" with God.

Another problem with this view is that many religious traditions hold that the good relationship with God is such that it is subject to *degree*. That is, there are degrees of the extent to which one can have a good relationship with God. A conception of the good relationship with God should have some way to account for this. But on the conception under consideration, there seems to be no way to do so. Radical union with God would have to be complete, not partial. One either has the good relationship with God (that is, union with God) totally, or one does not have it at all. The idea of being "partly identical" with God seems logically incoherent. Hence, the notion of radical union does not allow that there could be degrees of extent to which one has a good relationship with God. This is yet another reason for rejecting this conception.

Some advocates of radical union might respond that they are not concerned with what is "logical." But this book is an attempt to defend the rational defensibility of being religious. Those who endorse the notion of a relationship with God that is not logically coherent opt out of the claim that their position is rationally defensible.[59] For those of us interested in such a project, the notion of radical union must be rejected.

Conception 2: Obtaining Some Great Good Caused or Explained by God

On this alternative, the religious person seeks to obtain some great good, which is somehow caused or explained by God. This idea has roots in all of the major religious traditions.[60] There seems to be no *prima facie* incoherency in the idea that there be some great good which the religious theist might obtain that is in some way due to God. This is so whether God is conceived as a being with properties, or as Being, together with a set of divine principles.

If God is conceived as a being that is the causal source of the universe, then, given that God is conceived as metaphysically, intellectually, volitionally, and morally supreme, it seems eminently reasonable to think that God could cause the religious person to obtain some very great good which is better than anything else possible. We can make the same point, using more customary or traditional theological language. Suppose God is conceived as "omniscient" and "omnibenevolent". It seems reasonable to think that such a being would have the intelligence and power to cause the religious person to attain not just a very good state, but rather that state which is qualitatively the best kind one can possibly conceive.

Similarly, consider the alternative conception of God's ontological status. This conception has it that the world is designed in such a way that it operates in accord with certain fundamental divine principles. All of the natural or scientific laws of the cosmos are subsumed under principles such as maximal benevolence and maximal justice. It seems reasonable to think that the best kind of good attainable in such a world would be better than anything one could attain in any world in which these principles do not operate.

On either conception of God, the claim at stake is that only some good caused or explained by God could be the best kind of good for a human to obtain. But it is difficult to provide a formal proof for this claim. Suppose there is some possible kind of good which is qualitatively superior to any other kind of possible good. Now, suppose God could *not* cause that good. Would that entail an absurdity, namely, that God is less than omnipotent or omnibenevolent? It seems not. Suppose there is some *logical reason* for why

God couldn't cause that particular good. Set aside for the moment what that reason might be. If so, God's omnipotence would *not* be violated by the assumption that God cannot cause that good. For omnipotence does not require that God can do impossible things. Now, the question would be what logical reason could there be for why God couldn't cause that particular good? But how can we know whether there isn't some such reason? We cannot rule it out *a priori*. Therefore, we cannot give a formal proof for the desired claim.

Nevertheless, it still seems *plausible* to think that the best kind of good we could attain would be one that is caused or explained by a being or reality such as God. Although we cannot prove this *a priori*, so long as we have no positive reason to think there is some logical reason why God could *not* cause the best possible state, it is reasonable to think that God, and only God, can do so.

What might such a good state be like? It would seem plausible to view this good as infinite and unending, although possibly not static (that might be boring). Somewhat paradoxically perhaps, it is eminently reasonable also to admit that the *details* of this good might be difficult for us to fathom. Such a good might be something like heaven or bliss. While we may have only a vague idea about the content of heaven, it still seems reasonable to think that God would have sufficient power to arrange things in a way such that a qualitatively supreme kind of good is attainable for human beings.

It is also reasonable to conceive of this good in such a way that it is subject to *extent* or *degree*. That is, we may conceive of this good in such a way that different persons may attain to different degrees of this great good. Perhaps it's hard to fill in the details about what this might mean. But the idea seems coherent.

Surely, if there is some great good that God has in store for us, many of us would tend to think that such a good would come after death in some sort of future state. If we are trying to imagine the greatest good that a being such as God would be able to give us, many would be inclined to think that it would be everlasting. So, this view seems to require positing the possibility of a next world, or future state. While some may resist the notion of a future state as implausible, it is difficult to disprove this notion conclusively. There is no place here to enter a discussion of this issue. Suffice it to note that on many traditional accounts, this very special good is conceived as taking place in a next world.

A potential problem with this conception of the good relationship with God is that it seems to impute an impure or selfish motive to the religious life. For, on the present conception, the end goal of the religious life is to attain some special good that God has in store for us. As stated, it is usually conceived as a good that we can receive only in the next world. But if that is the religious goal, the religious person turns out to be someone who pursues a relationship with God for the sake of attaining a reward. As we saw, this point crops up in critical discussions of Pascal's Wager.[61] It is sometimes objected that, if the reason for believing in God is that it maximizes one's chances for attaining heavenly bliss, this seems to involve an impure or selfish motive for believing in God.

However, one response to this problem is the following.[62] Underlying the stated objection is the assumption that we can make a distinction between different kinds of value. We might put the point by saying that there is a distinction between *subjective* and *objective* value. (Those who find this distinction problematic will have difficulty formulating the objection in the first place.) A state or condition has *subjective* value if it involves or causes pleasure or joy for a given person. For example, having a relaxing massage, or even having a blissful spiritual experience has subjective value. On the other hand, a state has *objective* value if it involves or causes the goodness or well-being or flourishing of that person, not merely *qua* pleasure seeker, but *qua* human being.[63] Now, the objection as stated mistakenly assumes that the good attained in the next world is only a subjectively good state. If this were so, then perhaps it would be "selfish" to be religious just for the sake of attaining this type of good. But the religious theist may conceive of the good relationship with God as both subjectively and objectively valuable. In other words, he conceives of that relationship with God as not only one that involves or causes pleasure or joy; it also involves or causes the goodness, well-being or flourishing of the human being in the next world. If so, his religious life is not only or perhaps not primarily aimed at achieving a subjectively valuable good. It is aimed at achieving an objectively valuable good. Hence it is not a selfish endeavor after all.

Nevertheless, it still turns out that on this conception, the "good" that is involved in the good relationship with God is something *external* to God himself. Whether that "good" is subjective, objective, or a combination of both, it is still something *caused* or *explained* by God, and it is not God himself. Thus it still turns out that, on this conception, the religious person is pursuing a relationship with God for the sake of attaining some good *other than God*. This is one reason why the mystic prefers his version to this version. It would seem that the best and purest sort of good to pursue would be *God himself.* But we saw above that the option of mystical union is incoherent. So, if Conception 1 fails, how can *God himself* be the good that the religious person attains? One possible answer follows under Conception 3.

Conception 3: Interpersonal Bond

The conception of an interpersonal relationship or bond with God is found in all of the world's major theistic traditions. Typically this interpersonal bond is understood as a relationship of love and respect.[64] In a sense, this conception falls between the two conceptions discussed just above. As in the case of radical mystical union, the "good" which one attains on this conception is not something caused or explained by God, but rather, it is

God himself. By having this relationship with God, the religious person participates or shares in God's goodness. The notion of "participating" or "sharing" in God's goodness is not meant here to be taken lightly or metaphorically. The notion is that by attaining a certain relationship with God, one partakes of the divine goodness. Yet this conception must be sharply distinguished from the notion of radical union, which earlier we rejected as incoherent. In attaining the interpersonal bond with God, one does not thereby become *identical* with God.[65] Our task here is to articulate this concept.

It will be argued here that this is the best candidate for how to conceive coherently of the relationship with God as supremely valuable. Indeed, we will adopt this conception in the remainder of this book. However, let it be emphasized that the reader need not agree with this position in order to agree with the major argument of this book. What is necessary is that the reader agrees that there is *some* conception of the good relationship with God that is coherently conceived as supremely valuable. In any event, here we shall try to articulate the notion of an "interpersonal bond" with God in a broad way that any of the major theistic religions could accept. In the next part, we shall discuss some aspects that are particular to the Jewish conception of this relationship.

As stated, the interpersonal bond with God is a relationship of mutual *respect and love*. In what follows the aim is not to articulate a complete theory of love and respect, nor is it to attempt to describe all the possible different senses of these terms. Rather, the aim is to articulate what relationship a person might have with God in just such a way that one may be said to *partake* of God's supreme goodness. This is not to deny that there are other legitimate senses of *love* and *respect* that are not covered here. In passing, we shall also note some of the key differences between respect and love.

First, let us reiterate that this relationship is typically not conceived as something that the individual religious person can attain all on his own. This holds true in two ways. For one thing, the religious person's conception of God and the good relationship with God is such that God himself acts in such a way as to promote this type of relationship. Exactly how and under what circumstances God does this is another matter. But the religious person cannot succeed all on his own. Second, for most religions, the endeavor to attain and maintain this relationship is not conceived just as an individual project, but rather as a social project. The individual can truly bond with God only as part and parcel of a religious community that collectively bonds with God. There are several reasons for this; one is that this is just too difficult and complicated a task for one human being to do all on his own. We shall discuss this further (below in this section) and in our discussion (in Chapter 4) of Judaism, which strongly emphasizes the social nature of the good relationship with God.

Another preliminary: the present chapter aims to articulate a conception of a certain good relationship with God. In the next chapter we will discuss the conception of the religious *way*, that is, the conception of *how* one goes about trying to attain or maintain this relationship. But there need not be a hard and fast line between the relationship itself and the way to attain it. It is not surprising if the two conceptions are interdependent. We shall return to this point later. We now articulate the concepts of respect and love between the religious person and God.

Respect

Let x stand for some being, reality, person, or thing of any sort. To begin with, respect for x involves or presupposes a recognition or at least a belief about the *intrinsic value* or *worth* of x, *insofar as it is the kind of being or reality or thing that it is*. One can't genuinely respect someone or something unless one has some notion of its intrinsic worth or value. Of course, having the knowledge or belief that x is valuable does not *entail* that one will act respectfully toward x. Rather, such a recognition or belief is a necessary but not sufficient condition for respectful behavior toward x. Furthermore, respect is *proportionate* to the recognition or belief that some thing or being has intrinsic worth. There may be varying degrees to which different people recognize or believe in the value or worth of x, and so there may be varying degrees to which different people respect x. Finally, respect involves acting in whatever manner is appropriate toward x, insofar as x has the value or worth which it has. What actions are appropriate will of course depend on what x is, what value or worth x has, and other factors about how one stands in relationship to x.[66]

A clarification is necessary here about what kind of knowledge of or belief about x is required in order to have respect for x. We may distinguish *general* knowledge of or belief about x from *particular* or intimate knowledge of or beliefs about x. (There need not be a hard and fast line between general and particular knowledge in order to make this point.) To know or have beliefs about x in a general way is to have some knowledge or beliefs about the *kind* of being or reality x is. On the other hand, to know x or have beliefs about x in a particular way is to know or believe particular, distinctive facts about x that are not inferable from general knowledge of or beliefs about x. Thus for example, if I know you're a human being, and that is all I know about you, I have general knowledge of you. But if I know that you were born at a certain time and place, that you are five feet tall, have red hair, that you like chocolate, that you enjoy baseball, that you are feisty, loyal, good at math, and so on, then I have particular knowledge of you. These facts are not inferable from general knowledge or beliefs about you.

Only the general kind of knowledge of or beliefs about x is required for respect. All one needs to know about x in order to respect it is to know what kind of thing or being it is. Thus for example, if I know you are a human being, I ought to respect you as such, regardless of your particular traits. No closeness or kinship is required for respect. In fact, a person can be respected 'at a distance' so to speak. Indeed, respect might in some cases require *staying* at a distance from the object of respect. For example, a citizen of England might respect the Queen of England in a certain rather remote way. In addition, for respect to apply there need be little or no communication between the object of respect and the subject. However, communication *may* take place, and if so it may in part determine what is the appropriate, respectful way to act. For example, if the Queen commands certain things (that are within her dominion to command given her position), then respect will require doing those things. Thus, while particular knowledge of *x* is not necessary in order to have respect for *x*, the having of such knowledge may impact the form that respect for *x* takes.

Now, since God is conceived as *supreme*, respect for God involves recognition of the intrinsic value or worth of God *as supreme*. As stated earlier, God is metaphysically, volitionally, intellectually, and morally supreme. For many religions, there are several ways in which respect for God is expressed or played out. Primarily, respect for God involves a certain kind of *awe* or *reverence* on the part of the religious person. Awe or reverence is an emotion, which is fitting to have with respect to the Supreme Person.[67] Second, as in the case of the Queen described above, should one come to believe or know that not only is there a God but also that God wishes, or even more so, commands, that one do or avoid certain things, respect would involve *obedience* to God's wishes or commands. The willingness to obey God's commands is also a form of *worship*. However, the point still stands that one need only have a general knowledge of or beliefs about God in order to be in a position to respect God. All one needs to know is what *kind* of being or reality God is. One need not have particular knowledge or beliefs about what God has done or said in order to have respect for God.[68]

So far we have discussed what it means for a human person to respect God. What might it mean for God to have *respect* for a person? We may articulate this as follows. For God to respect a person would mean for God to recognize one's intrinsic worth as a person and treat him or her accordingly. Since God is conceived as morally supreme, God is conceived in such a way that he does respect persons insofar as they are persons. But what is involved in God's treating us accordingly? One thing it might mean is that God treats us as responsible moral agents. In simple terms, God is not unfair to us. Another thing it might mean is that he gives us responsibilities and holds us accountable for our actions. He rewards and punishes us according to our merits. Perhaps it also means that God manages the world (or, on the alternative conception, the world is structured by the divine principles) in just such a way that is conducive to our moral growth or maturity over the course of time. There may be more involved in God's respect for persons than this, but this will suffice for the present purpose.

Love

As stated earlier, there are many different senses of the term "love". Our aim here is to articulate one sense of that term. To begin with, we may say that love of *x* involves recognition of or belief in the intrinsic value or worth of *x*, *insofar as it is the particular being or reality that it is*. One cannot genuinely love something or someone unless one has some idea of the value or worth of *x as an individual*. Now, love of *x* requires, as a prerequisite, respect for *x*. For in order to know and appreciate what *x* is as an individual, one must also know and appreciate what kind of being or reality *x* is. But whereas respect requires only a general recognition of the intrinsic value of *x* insofar as it is a certain *kind* of being or reality, love requires a more particular recognition of the value of *x* insofar as it is a *particular* or *individual* being or reality. And, as in the case of respect, the degree of one's love for *x* will be proportionate to the degree of one's recognition of the worth or value of *x*. Again, there are senses of the term "love" for which none of all this holds. It is possible to use the word "love" in such a way that one means something rather different than what is intended here.

Furthermore, unlike respect, love involves the desire to establish a certain intimacy with *x*. Love requires the development of a certain closeness or kinship. Communication is also required. Two persons who do not communicate or know each other very well cannot be truly said to love each other very well. The more intense the closeness and the more direct is the communication, the more intense may the love be. Earlier we distinguished between general knowledge or beliefs about x, and, particular knowledge or beliefs about *x*. For love of *x*, one must have at least some particular knowledge of *x*. The more particular knowledge or belief one has, the more one is in a position to love *x*. Again, such particular knowledge or belief will not *entail* the presence of love. It is a necessary but not sufficient condition for it.

What is involved in an intimate relationship with God other than communication, and knowledge? Whereas respect for God involves dread and awe, love on the other hand elicits a more positive kind of response. The details of course will depend on one's religion. However, the following two things are espoused by many religious traditions. The first involves what is sometimes referred to as *walking in God's way*. Since God is conceived as having a morally supreme personality or character, to *walk in God's way* is, among other things, to think, act, and speak in a morally upright manner. What this involves in more detail and how precisely one does this will vary from religion to religion. But the basic idea is the same. By walking in God's way, one relates to God and one allows God to express himself more fully within one's life (on this notion see below).

Second, since God is supreme, love of God involves a willingness to obey whatever God wishes or commands, if one should come to know or believe that God wishes or commands certain things. (The question of how one might know that God exists or what God wishes or commands is not relevant at the moment.) The lover seeks to do the will of the beloved. Again, this is what we might call *worship* or service of God. It is through worship also that one becomes close to God. Earlier we mentioned that respect for God calls forth obedience. The willingness to serve God stems from both respect and love.

It's worth noting that neither of these things are necessarily a part of what love would entail *between humans*. When you love someone such as a child, spouse, or friend, you do not necessarily set out either to "walk in their way," or to worship or obey them. Of course, they might happen to have a character trait that you admire or think is worthy of developing, but to say that you are setting out to imitate them in order to develop it would still be mistaken, by and large. And, while you may under certain circumstances "obey" your spouse or friend and especially your parent, this is still not the same as *worship*. (We do sometimes speak of a lover as "worshipping" his beloved, but that is a metaphor or exaggeration.) Basically, the difference stems not from the fact that the *kind* of love for God is different from the *kind* of love we might have for other humans, but rather from the fact that God is supreme whereas other persons are not. Further discussion of this issue is not necessary for the present purpose.

How does God express love for the religious person? We may articulate this in a way analogous to what was said above regarding God's respect for the religious person. On the standard conception, God loves the religious person insofar as God participates in his or her life, and helps him or her to walk in God's way.[69] God does not leave the religious person up to his own devices, so to speak, in the latter's spiritual quest. This is so in two ways. First, God causes certain events to happen which promote the religious person's quest to walk in God's way. More deeply, though, God loves the religious person insofar as God imbues him or her with the divine character. God shapes and molds the religious person's personality so that the religious person succeeds in walking along God's way.[70]

On the alternative conception, one needs to put this point differently, but it comes to much the same thing, namely, that the religious person is not "left to his own devices" in the quest to relate well with God. God's love for the religious person consists in that the divine principles are such that the person's efforts to conform his or her behavior to them are facilitated by those principles. Events happen in the world that are conducive to the religious person's walking in God's way. The religious person's personality is molded and shaped so that he may succeed in walking along God's way.

Some may be inclined to worry that there is a danger of incoherency lurking here, for we seem to be saying that God's love for the religious person involves God's tinkering with his freedom or personhood, which would seem to violate God's respect for the person. God cannot overwhelm the person with his own divine character, for then, that person's "walking in God's way" would itself not be free and therefore would not be as divine as it might be. However, an analogy may be made to the case of a parent who teaches a child moral values. A good parent shows her child the way and nurtures the child's moral growth, without overwhelming the child so as to lose his autonomy. It is the task of philosophical theology to work out further details of the interplay between divine action and human autonomy.[71]

So much for a brief account of respect and love. These are the two key elements in the interpersonal bond with God. On this conception, we can make ample sense of the idea that this relationship admits of *degrees*. There are degrees of the extent to which a person may bond with God. For, there are degrees of the extent to which a person may love and respect God, and there are degrees of extent to which God may respect and love the religious person. Furthermore, earlier we distinguished between subjective and objective value. The religious theist may conceive of the bond with God as both subjectively and objectively valuable. In other words, having that bond with God not only involves or causes pleasure or joy; it also involves or causes the well-being or flourishing of the human being.

This view has at least one advantage over the previous conception. On the second option above, one pursues a relationship with God in order to attain that great good that God will bestow. It turns out that the good which one pursues as a religious person is something *other than God himself*. But on the present conception, the religious person's goal is to attain a bond or intimate connection with God. Now, the person who does this may very well know or believe that by doing so, he thereby pursues a very valuable state. But the good that such a person pursues is ultimately *God himself*, and not something caused or explained by God such as heaven or bliss.

On either ontological conception of God, this notion is coherent. However, one reason for thinking it makes more sense on the alternative than on the standard conception is the following. On the standard conception, God is conceived as a being with certain properties. God is a being external to us. If so, our relationship with God will always be in some way mediated. On the conception of God as *a being*, it seems the best one could do is *imitate* God, and thereby attain some kind of goodness that is *like* God's goodness, rather than actually *partake* of God's goodness itself. Of course, one could respect and love God. One could act in a Godly manner; one could act in accord with God's will. But how would that create a *bond* or *union* between oneself and God, except in a kind of loose or metaphorical sense?

However, on the alternative conception, God's essence is Being, and God's attributes are understood as certain principles in accord with which the world operates. God's personhood and personality are understood in terms of certain divine principles that structure the world. On this view, God's essence is not a being outside of us. God's essence is in some sense already expressed within us. Furthermore, on this view, the relationship of bonding may be understood as follows. In general, when one acts in a certain way, one conforms one's behavior to certain principles. Suppose one chooses to live in accord with the divine principles described above, to the greatest extent that one can. By living a certain way of life, by conforming our behavior to the divine principles, one would thereby more fully manifest and express Being, that is, God, in the world. As stated earlier, God is also involved in this project, in that the principles themselves are such that our own efforts to conform our behavior to the divine principles are facilitated by events that happen in the world. One can then, quite literally bond with God's personhood/personality. One thereby partakes of God's supreme goodness. Of course, to bond with God's personality and personhood is *not* to become identical with the essence of God, nor with the principles that constitute God's personhood and personality. Rather, to bond with God's personhood and personality is to behave in such a way that one manifests or expresses those principles in one's own personality.

So much for an articulation of the notion of the bond with God. It is rationally defensible to think that an interpersonal relationship of the sort described with the Supreme Person would be supremely worthwhile for the human person having that relationship. Inasmuch as God is conceived as supreme, the relationship of bonding with God is plausibly conceived by the religious theist as having supreme worth or value for the religious person. For, in that relationship, the religious person bonds with God's very personality/personhood, and therefore *shares* or *participates* in God's goodness. Thus the good relationship with God is conceived not merely as "a lot better" or "vastly better" than any other goal, but as qualitatively superior to any other goal. Differently stated, the religious goal is conceived as better not in quantity but in kind than any other conceivable good a human might have; no quantitative amount of other goods (that is, goods that a human might have independently of a good relationship with God) added together would equal the value of that relationship for that human.

We have argued that the conception of the good relationship with God as an interpersonal bond is coherent and that it is rationally defensible to conceive of such a relationship as supremely valuable. In spite of the account offered above of respect and love, the details of what is involved in a good relationship with God have been left open. Different religions (and different theologians within the same religion) will fill in these details in different and sometimes sharply contrasting ways.

If a person has this conception of a good relationship with God, what follows about his commitments regarding alternative conceptions of the good relationship with God, and, for that matter, regarding non-theistic conceptions of the goal of human life? No doubt, he will find *some* competing conceptions to be incoherent. However, in order for it to be rationally defensible for him to have the conception that he has, he need not think that his own conception is the *only* coherent one. We shall return to this issue later.

3.4 The Conception of the Religious Way

The "religious way" is the means by which the religious person pursues the good relationship with God. It is rationally defensible for a person to have a certain conception of the religious way if it is internally coherent, and if it fits or coheres with the other relevant concepts, namely, one's conception of God and the good relationship with God. To show that some conception of the religious way is coherent, one needs to articulate it in a coherent way, and to show how the way fits with the end. The more one can do this, the better.

The aim of the present chapter is to articulate, in broad strokes, a coherent conception of the religious way. The conception proposed here contains elements possessed in common by several (though not necessarily all) theistic religions. However, the proposal here is in an important sense unfinished or open-ended. Like our articulation of the conceptions of God and the good relationship with God in the previous chapters, much room will be left open on how to fill in important details regarding the religious way. Nevertheless, there is no reason in principle to think that this couldn't be done. In fact, there will be many different yet internally coherent ways of filling in those details. In the next chapter, we shall describe and critically discuss the Jewish conception of the religious way, which may be viewed as one particular way of filling in the details of the broad conception offered in this section.

In the previous section (3.3), we suggested that a good relationship with God is best conceived as an interpersonal bond with God, one that is constituted by mutual love and respect. It follows that the religious way will consist in the effort to attain or maintain that relationship. For the sake of convenience, let us say that the religious way includes *religious actions*, that is, actions that are supposed to promote the good relationship with God. The term "actions" here is intended in the broadest sense, including, for example, physical behaviors such as rituals, taboos, mores, and so on, but also verbal practices and even thoughts. Our question may now be restated: *what actions might plausibly be regarded as religious actions?*

Spiritual Activities

There are basically two ways in which some action or set of actions might plausibly be regarded as *religious*. First, given the conceptions of God and the good relationship with God articulated in the previous sections, one may plausibly infer that certain actions count as religious. Under this heading, two major categories may be mentioned. Since the relationship of mutual respect and love ideally involves knowledge of God, it follows that actions that promote knowledge or intimacy with God are plausibly conceived as part of the religious life. What might such actions be? At the very least, such actions would include what might be called spiritual activities, such as *contemplation*, *meditation*, and *prayer*.

A detailed account of these notions is beyond our scope. No doubt these terms are used in a variety of ways. For the present purpose, *contemplation* of God involves thinking discursively (critically, analytically or philosophically) about God, God's nature and attributes, and so on. *Meditation* involves focusing the mind on God or on the idea of God in a non-discursive or non-analytic fashion.[72] Prayer involves petitioning God for something. In this context, the most relevant petition would be *asking God to relate to us well and to help us relate to him well*. One can also pray more generally for success in the spiritual path. Now it is plausible to think that, if there were a God of the sort described above, such activities would bring the religious person toward a more intimate relationship with God. After all, God is conceived as a Supreme Person, who understands prayer and is capable of communication. It is not surprising that such activities are common to all theistic traditions.

Walking in God's Way: Moral Behavior

Second, given that God is conceived as morally supreme, and the good relationship with God consists at least partly in "walking in God's way," it follows that living a moral life is plausibly considered part of the religious life. Thus, for the religious theist, the moral life is part and parcel of the religious way. The moral life is not merely a means to a religious end, it is part of the end itself. Incidentally, this does not commit us to saying that one couldn't be moral without being religious. There is no claim here that the *only* reason to live a moral life is if it fits into a religious life. However, in the context of a religious way of life, moral behavior has an added significance that it does not have on a purely secular or non-religious approach.

Following a Divinely Revealed Way: Study and Practice

So far we have mentioned two categories of religious actions that one may plausibly infer from the conceptions of God and the good relationship with God. In addition, as is the case in many actual religions (including the biblically based ones), the religious way may include certain actions that are based on some empirical or factual claim(s). Typically this involves a claim that God has revealed or communicated certain directives about how to live, and about how to attain a good relationship with God. A religious way may include, for example, certain practices that are purported to be revealed by God as a means of attaining a good relationship with him. In many cases, such a practice may not be inferable from the concept of God or the good relationship with God as articulated above. The only way it is known, if it is known at all, is through divine revelation.

The issue of whether such claims about revelation can be justified or rationally defended is not relevant to our discussion at present. Our concern in this section is only with what makes for a conceptually coherent religious way, not necessarily a "true" or valid one. Now, we have already argued (above in Section 3.2) that the notion of divine revelation or divine communication itself is coherent. The present issue is whether it is conceptually plausible to think that the religious way would include following certain divinely revealed directives. A little reflection shows it is eminently plausible to think so.

Let us reiterate a point made earlier in the discussion of the conception of God. God is conceived in such a way that there is a high *a priori* probability that if there is a God, then God will reveal himself and seek to establish a relationship with other persons. And so, even though it is not *necessary* that God do these things (for that would be to deny God's freedom) it is *reasonable* to *expect* that (if there is a God) he would, at some point in human history, engage humans in this project. Hence, it should not surprise us if a conception of the religious way involves certain practices that rest on claims about God's revelation or purported revelation. (Again, whether such claims can be justified or rationally defended is a separate problem. See discussion of this in the next section.) It should also not surprise us if some of those practices are *not* inferable from the concepts of God and the good relationship with God. Indeed, such practices might include things that are "mysteries" and make no apparent sense to us at all. After all, God is conceived as supremely intelligent, and he may very well know all sorts of things about how we should act that we would never imagine.[73]

Of course, precisely what those practices are differs from one religion to the next. Obviously, that is partly because different religions make different claims about the content of God's revelation. But, broadly speaking, for those religions that involve some claim of divine revelation or communication, the religious way tends to include at least two categories of actions. These two categories parallel the two categories mentioned earlier regarding what can be plausibly inferred from the conceptions of God and the good relationship with God. These include first, actions aimed at knowing or being intimate with God through the study of God's revelation, whatever form that might take, such as scripture, oral tradition, and so on. Thus, most religions that involve revelation include "study of holy scripture" in some form as an integral part of the religious way. The second category includes acting in accord with God's revealed directives about how to attain the good relationship with God. Such directives may include certain ritual practices, but also ones that encourage or deepen the moral life, as well as directives about how to contemplate and pray, and so on. In other words, the revealed directives may shape and guide those religious actions which one would have inferred (without revelation) from the concepts of God and the good relationship with God.

In summary, a conception of the religious way is plausible if it is internally coherent and if it fits with the conception of God and the good relationship with God. Given the conception of the good relationship with

God as an interpersonal bond, one would plausibly expect a religious way to include a) spiritual activities such as meditation, contemplation, and prayer; and b) moral behavior. In addition, a given religious way may invoke some claim about God's revelation or purported revelation. For a religious way that does invoke such a claim, one may plausibly expect such a conception to include at least c) study of God's revelation; and, d) acting in accord with God's revealed directives about how to live rightly and about how to attain the good relationship with God. In principle, there is no reason to think that there couldn't be many different conceptually plausible religious ways that differ in their details. The closer or tighter is the fit between a given religious way and a given detailed conception of the good relationship with God, the more plausible is it to think of that religious way as a means toward that goal.

Aside from the fact that different religious ways rest on different empirical claims about God's revelations, it is also the case that different religious ways tend to emphasize different aspects of a)–d) above. Even within the same religion, some theologians or religious thinkers tend to emphasize different aspects of the religious way. Some will claim that the activities that make sense *a priori*, that is, those described under a) and b), are more important than any revealed information, that is, c) and d). But some will claim the opposite. Regarding the relationship of intimacy itself, some will emphasize the intellectual aspects, while others emphasize the emotional or "spiritual" aspects. We need not here enter such debates.

It will be useful to describe briefly what a *non*-religious (or at least, non-theistically religious) way of life is. First, a non-religious person could conceivably have a belief, even a confident belief, that there is a God. However, a non-religious way of life would be any way of life that does *not* involve the pursuit of a good relationship with God. A non-religious person might engage in certain activities that are similar in certain respects to the actions of a religious person, but they would not be done with the same intent or aspirations. He might think about the idea of God, for example, but we would not call that contemplation or meditation on God. He might live a moral life, but not as part and parcel of an effort to relate well with God. He might study texts that are purported to be revealed, but not as part of an effort to find out what God wishes. It goes without saying that it is *not* conceptually plausible to think of a non-religious way of life as a means to the religious goal.

What, if anything, is the religious theist committed to regarding *alternative* conceptions of the religious way other than his own? As we shall see later, this question becomes important when we turn to the issue of whether it is rationally defensible for a person to choose a particular religious way *as opposed to* some other competing way. If a person thinks a certain way is conceptually plausible, that does not mean he is committed to thinking that other ways are *not* plausible. Certainly, he may (and should) admit that if the good relationship with God is conceived in a *different* way than he conceives it, then some alternative religious way may very well make more sense as a means toward *that* end. For example, suppose one person conceives of the good relationship with God as consisting in mutual love and respect, while someone else conceives of it as some form of masochistic relationship. The first person will (and should) readily concede that a masochistic religious way that, for example, emphasizes certain self-flagellating practices would be more plausible (than is his own religious way) as a means toward *that* masochistic end!

However, could the religious theist admit that some alternative religious way could just as easily be a *means* toward the end *as he conceives it*? As far as anything we have said so far goes, he might very well think so. However, under some circumstances, it might turn out that compared with his own religious way, *no* alternative religious way is as plausible as a means to the end *as he conceives it*. Whether this is so will depend partly on 1) how richly detailed is his conception of God and the good relationship with God, and 2) how close or tight is the "fit" between his own religious way and the conception of the good relationship with God as he conceives it. The more 1) and 2) are true, the less plausible will any alternative religious way be as a means toward that end as he conceives it. The more richly detailed is his conception of the end, and the closer the fit is between his conceptions of the way and the end, the less reasonable will it be to think that some alternative is just as plausible as a means to that end. We shall return to this issue later.

3.5 The Belief in the Live Possibility of God

Next, the religious theist must have the belief that there is (at least) a live possibility that there is a God. To have this belief is stronger than merely to have the conception of God. Under what circumstances would it be rationally defensible for a person to have this belief? In general, under what circumstances is it rationally defensible for someone to believe there is at least a live possibility that some proposition *p* is true?

As stipulated earlier,[74] to believe there is a live possibility that *p* is to not be totally convinced that *p* is false, and to be disposed, at least under some hypothetical circumstances, to take *p* into account when deciding how to act. The following criterion seems plausible. If 1) it is rationally defensible to believe there is (at least) some small evidence that *p* is true, and, 2) it is rationally defensible to believe there is no conclusive proof that *p* is false, then it is rationally defensible to believe that there is (at least) a live possibility that *p* is true. Stated more simply, as long as I have some reason to think *p* is true, and no definitive proof that *p* is false, then it is rationally defensible for me to believe there is a live possibility that *p*.

To illustrate the use of the criterion, take the following example. Consider the belief that *there is a live possibility that there is intelligent extra-*

terrestrial life. Under what circumstances would it be rationally defensible
to have this belief? The claim here is that it is rationally defensible to have
this belief if a) there is some small evidence for it, and, b) there is no
compelling evidence against it. If there were some small evidence for it, one
would be well disposed to take it into account when acting; and, if there is
no compelling disproof, one is justified in not being convinced that it is
false.

Based on this two-fold criterion, many will agree that it is rationally
defensible to believe there is (at least) a live possibility that there is a God
of the sort described above, that is, a Supreme Person. First, even many an
atheist (and surely, many an agnostic) admits there is (at least) some
evidence that there is a God. That evidence includes the various religious
traditions that purport that God, the Supreme Person, has revealed himself
to human beings. To see that this is correct, imagine a world in which no one
ever claimed to have experienced God, and no one ever claimed that God
had revealed himself. All other things being equal, a person living in such a
world would have *less* evidence to believe that there is a God than a person
living in our world, where many people have made this claim. If this is right,
it follows that there is at least some small evidence for God's existence or
reality in our world.[75]

Note well: there is no claim here that putative religious experience and
reports of revelation, nor any of the other arguments provide *compelling*
reason for the belief that there is a God. In fact, there is no claim here that
the evidence supports the proposition that there is a probability greater than
half that there is a God. The latter claim is made by philosophers who
support the "argument from religious experience."[76] Critics dismiss the
evidence as delusional or fabricated, or just plain insufficient to establish
that there is a probability greater than half that there is a God. It is not within
the scope of this book to enter this debate. However, even many of those
who dispute the argument from religious experience will not deny that there
is *at least some small evidence* that there is a God. Hence, the first criterion
above is met.

Second, let us consider a person who is well aware of the standard
critiques (based on Hume, Freud, and so on) against the belief in God.
Despite such critiques, very few philosophers claim that there is *definitive
proof* that there is no God. Perhaps the most popular argument against the
existence of God is based on the problem of evil. But it is notoriously hard
to show that the existence of evil is logically incompatible with God.[77] There
are various theories on why the Supreme Person might have some legitimate
reason for allowing evil. In fact, there are many atheists (and of course,
many agnostics) who would concede that there is no definitive proof against
God's reality or existence. Rather, they tend to claim that God's existence is
unlikely.[78] Hence the second part of the criterion is also met. In sum, it is
rationally defensible for many persons to believe there is a live possibility
that there is a God. Again, this still leaves open whether it is rationally

defensible to believe there is anything *more* than a live possibility that there is a God. That brings up the more standard project in the philosophy of religion, which is not the subject of this book.[79]

An important qualifying point needs to be made. We have argued that it is rationally defensible to believe there is at least a live possibility that there is a God. But our argument here is only for the minimal belief under the general conception of God described above. To the extent that a person adds to the basic concept of God certain specific features, his belief that there is a live possibility that such a God exists will need more evidentiary support. Again, for a minimal belief, it will not need *much* support (only some evidence and no compelling evidence against it). We shall revisit this point in the next chapter.

3.6 The Belief that Following a Certain Religious Way Promotes the Good Relationship with God

As noted earlier,[80] it is not sufficient for the religious theist to believe *only* that there is a plausible fit between his conceptions of God, the good relationship with God, and the way to attain that relationship. In addition, he is committed to the belief that the probability that he will attain or maintain that relationship is (at least slightly) higher if he follows a certain religious way than if he does not.

At issue here is the religious person's belief that there is a higher probability that he will attain the relationship with God by following a certain religious way *rather than by not being religious at all*. Later we shall consider the rationality of the belief that there is a higher probability that he will attain the relationship by following a certain religious way *rather than by following some other religious way*.

Let us assume that a person has a conception of the religious way of the typical sort described earlier. Generally, such a religious way will include a) cognitive/spiritual activities such as meditation, contemplation, and prayer; and b) moral behavior. In addition, a religious way may rest on a claim regarding some purported divine revelation. Typically, such a religious way will include c) study of God's revelation; and d) following God's revealed directives about how to live rightly and about how to attain and maintain the good relationship with God. We have already argued that such a conception is plausible. Our question now is, under what circumstances would it be rationally defensible for a person to believe that following a certain religious way increases (at least slightly) the probability that he will attain or maintain a good relationship with God?

The answer to this question is complicated by the fact that whereas components a) and b) do not (necessarily) rest on a claim of specific revelation, c) and d) do depend on some claim of revelation. Regarding components a) and b) of *any* religious way, the following argument may be given. We have already claimed that 1) it is rationally defensible to believe there is at least some small evidence that there is a God and 2) it is more *conceptually plausible* that one will attain the good relationship with God if one engages in a) and b) than if one does not. It follows that it is rationally defensible to believe it is *more probable* that one will attain the good relationship with God if one engages in a) and b) than if one does not.

To see this point, consider the following analogy. Assume that 1) there is a *live possibility* that there is friendly intelligent extraterrestrial life in outer space. Now suppose we have the goal of communicating with such extraterrestrial beings, should they happen to exist. Assume also that 2) it is more conceptually plausible that we will communicate with them if we send out intelligent signals into outer space than if we do not. Such an assumption may rest on our conception of intelligent creatures, and our conception of what it means to "communicate."[81] Given 1) and 2), it follows that it is *more probable* that we will communicate with them if we send out signs of intelligent communication than if we do not.[82] Similarly, so long as there is some live possibility that there is a God, it is rationally defensible to believe it is *more probable* that one will attain or maintain the good relationship with God if one engages in a) and b) than if one does not.

However, the actions under c) and d) stem from some purported divine revelation. Call that purported revelation *R*. Even if there is evidence that there is a God, it does not directly follow that one has any reason to believe that engaging in the actions recommended by *R* increases the probability that one will attain the good relationship with God. For even if there is a God, *R* could be utterly fictitious or inauthentic.

But suppose one had at least some small evidence that *R* actually occurred and was an authentic revelation of God's will. And suppose one had no compelling evidence that *R* did *not* occur. Suppose also that given the person's conception of the good relationship with God, the *only* way he or she can attain it, if at all, is through the religious way that is based on *R*. Under these circumstances it would be rationally defensible for him to believe that engaging in the actions based on that revelation increase, at least slightly, the probability that one will attain that relationship with God.

To see this point, consider the following analogy. Suppose I wish to own a million dollars. Suppose also that there is (at least) some (slight) probability that if I buy certain lottery ticket I will win and make a million dollars. Suppose I have determined that if I am ever going to make a million dollars, it is *only* by winning the lottery. In other words, buying the ticket might bring about my goal of making a million. And, it can't hurt. It follows that my chances of making a million dollars are at least slightly higher if I buy the ticket than if I do not.

Similarly, it is rationally defensible to believe that engaging in the actions based on a certain revelation *R* increase, at least slightly, the probability that one will attain the good relationship with God if[83] it is rationally defensible to believe:

1 there is at least some slight evidence that R occurred, and,
2 there is no compelling evidence that R did not occur, and,
3 the *only* way he or she can attain a certain relationship with God is through following the way based on *R*.

This leads naturally to the question, under what circumstances is it rationally defensible to believe 1) there is at least some slight evidence that revelation *R* occurred, and 2) no compelling evidence that *R* did not occur?

Generally, a claim to the effect that some revelation *R* occurred is based on a claim that someone (or some group of persons) has had an *experience* that *R* occurred. If I myself have had such an experience, or if people I know and trust claim to have had a certain experience, I have at least *some* evidence that such a revelation occurred. To be sure, skeptical arguments against revelation can be made. There seem to be many conflicting "revelations"; perhaps this casts doubt on the veracity of all of them. Which purported revelation, if any, is authentic or veridical? Despite these worries, in general, the circumstances under which there is *some* slight evidence for a given revelation *R*, and no *compelling disproof* of it are not too difficult to be obtained. In the next part we shall set forth this argument in the case of Judaism. But it could easily be done for other religions as well.

Meanwhile, let us turn to condition 3). Under what circumstances is it rationally defensible to think that 3) the *only* way a person can attain a certain relationship with God is through following the way based on *R*? This brings us back to a point stated at the end of Section 3.4. Suppose a person's particular conceptions of God and the good relationship with God are richly detailed, and that there is a tight fit between his conception of the religious way and his conception of the religious goal. In that case, it may turn out that a certain religious way is the *only* conceptually plausible way as means to the end *as he conceives it*. This is the argument made in the next chapter regarding Judaism. But, in principle, it is not hard to make this argument in the case of other religions as well.

There is another way in which one could have at least some evidence that certain actions, whether or not they are based on a claim of revelation, promote the relationship with God. Suppose I find certain persons who seem, of all the people I know, to be the most likely to have a certain good relationship with God, if indeed there is a God at all. By considering their actions, I may come to formulate some reasonable conclusions about what actions are the most likely to promote the religious goal. After all, it is an empirical fact that of all those people who are candidates for having the relationship with God, those who behave in certain typically religious ways are by far the more likely to be people that actually have the relationship. This constitutes some evidence that the most likely way of attaining a good relationship with God is by following a religious way.

To see this point better, imagine a world in which people who have been *non*-religious all of their lives suddenly claim to have a good interpersonal relationship with God. What would be weirder still, imagine that such people *recommended* that the best way to attain such a relationship is by *not* being religious! If we lived in such a world, we would be entitled to believe that *not* following a religious way is more likely to result in a good relationship with God than doing so. But our world – the actual world – is not like that. It is an empirical fact that almost no one claims to have attained a good relationship with God by *not* being religious. Even those who make the claim that they have attained a good relationship with God without previously being religious (as in the case of sudden conversion) are not likely to *recommend* this as the most likely way to attain the good relationship with God. Hence, in our world, we do have at least some evidence to believe that we are (at least slightly) more likely to attain a good relationship with God by following a religious way than by not doing so.

In summary of this section, a typical religious way includes various kinds of actions. Some of those actions (spiritual and meditative practices, and moral behavior) are inherently plausible as means to the religious end. Given that there is (at least some slight) evidence that there is a God, it is rationally defensible to believe that engaging in those actions will increase (at least slightly) the probability that the good relationship with God is attained. There is also support "from the field" that these activities promote a good relationship with God (if there is a God at all). Other actions in a typical religious way (for example, rituals) may rest on a specific claim of revelation, or on other empirical claims regarding certain religious persons. It is rationally defensible to believe that such actions increase the probability of attaining the good relationship with God to the extent that there is some evidence for that claim of revelation or for those empirical claims, and to the extent that the religious way in question is the only plausible way to attain that relationship. In the next chapter it will be argued that these constraints are met in the case of Judaism. That result will not preclude others from arguing that they are also met in the case of other religions.

Finally, what view is the religious theist committed to regarding competing religious ways *other than his own*? Certainly, he can (and should) admit that on some *alternative* conception of God or the good relationship with God other than his own, it may very well be the case that some *alternative* religious way is more likely (than his own) to result in *that* relationship. But, could he be in the position of believing that some alternative way is just as likely, or perhaps even more likely *than his own* religious way, to result in the good relationship with God *as he conceives it*? If he does, then his commitment to his own religious way as opposed to that alternative may not be rationally defensible. We shall return to this point later.

3.7 Following a Religious Way (Doing Those Actions Which One Believes Promote the Good Relationship with God)

The final condition for being a religious theist is that one must engage in those actions which one believes will promote the probability of attaining or maintaining the good relationship with God. To ask whether it is rationally defensible to fulfill this condition is to ask whether it is rational to engage in a certain course of action. The adoption of a course of action may be evaluated on pragmatic grounds, that is, on the basis of whether it is potentially more valuable to engage in that course of action than not to do so. In what follows, it will be argued on pragmatic grounds that, so long as certain constraints are met, it is rationally defensible to follow a religious way of life. First, it is necessary to revisit the Expected Value Principle.

Application of the Expected Value Principle: The Case of Dan and Rebecca

Given a set of options and potential outcomes, the Expected Value Principle provides a mechanism for "weighting" the values of potential outcomes on various options, and comparing these weighted values. It is worth noting that the Expected Value Principle may be applied in cases where it may be difficult to assign specific numerical measurements for probability and value assignments. The following example illustrates this point.

Suppose Dan is courting a certain Rebecca. Dan regards her as exquisitely beautiful, noble, and uniquely gifted. Dan thinks it is very unlikely that he will ever meet another woman quite like Rebecca. Assume also that Dan thinks his chance of success at winning Rebecca's hand is very low. Now suppose Dan is faced with the decision of continuing to pursue Rebecca or not. The Expected Value Principle will yield that it is rational for Dan to pursue Rebecca, so long as he deems the value of success to be high enough, relative to the other goals attainable on his other available options. In general, the more value he attaches to winning Rebecca's hand, the less likely must he deem the chances for success in order for it to be rational for him to make the effort to do so. Dan's case may be represented by formulating the following options:

Option A: Make every effort to win Rebecca's hand.

Option B: Do not make every effort to win Rebecca's hand.

For the sake of discussion, suppose Dan believes that on Option A he has only a 1/10 chance of success, and a 9/10 chance of failure. Set aside, for the moment, how Dan made these estimations. If the value of success is represented by some very high number S and the value of failure is zero, then the expected value of option A is:

$$(1/10 \times S) + (9/10 \times 0) = S/10$$

On the other hand, suppose Dan believes Option B has 99/100 chance of resulting in some moderate value M. This may be because Dan thinks that, by not bothering to pursue Rebecca, he may successfully pursue some other woman who is not, in his estimation, as precious as her. To make the case more interesting, suppose that even on Option B there is some small chance that Rebecca may turn around and fall in love with Dan. That is, there is some very chance that *not* making the effort will actually help his cause. Let us also suppose that Dan is reasonable enough to allow some very small chance that someone else may come along who is just as precious as Rebecca. So, let's say that the chance of his attaining S on Option B is 1/100. The expected value of option B is:

$$99/100 \times M + 1/100 \times S = (99 \times M) / 100 + S/100$$

Given these results, it follows that Option A will have a higher expected value than Option B if and only if:

$$S/10 > (99 \times M) / 100 + S/100$$

Solving for S, the expected value of Option A will be higher than that of Option B, so long as:

$$S > M \times 11$$

Now in real life, it might be difficult for Dan to determine whether S is worth more than 11 times M. It also might be difficult to determine or even guess the probability of success or failure on Option A. So, if Dan thinks that S is just "a lot better" than M, then he might not be able to make a rational decision based on the Expected Value Principle. But if he thinks that S *vastly overwhelms M*, and that the probability that he will attain S on Option A is higher than it is on Option B, then the Expected Value of Option A will be higher than that of Option B.

An important caveat about expected value assessments must be noted. An action may have a high expected value for a given person, *given* the beliefs and value assignments of that person. Of course, that does not in itself imply that the action is rationally defensible, *unless the beliefs and value assignments upon which that assessment is based are also rationally defensible*. For example, suppose Dan has deluded himself into thinking that he has *any chance whatsoever* of successfully winning Rebecca's hand. Alternatively, suppose Dan has an exaggerated conception of how precious is Rebecca relative to other women. In this case, the calculation that Option A has a higher expected value does not yield the result that it is rationally defensible, since Dan's premises are not rationally defensible. In general, an expected value assessment shows that it is rationally defensible to do some action only if the beliefs and value assignments upon which that assessment is made are also rationally defensible.

The Decision About Whether to Follow a Religious Way

Now let us return to the decision problem at issue in this book. As argued in the previous sections of this chapter, so long as certain constraints are met, it is rationally defensible for a person to fulfill all the conditions heretofore described for being a religious theist. Such a person has a rationally defensible belief that there is (at least) a live possibility that there is a God, and that he is more likely to attain a good relationship with God by following a certain religious way than by not doing so. Furthermore, such a person conceives of the good relationship with God as supremely valuable, that is, qualitatively superior to any other goal. The decision problem he now faces is, should he follow that religious way of life, or not?

This decision problem is analogous to that of Dan in the case described above. He may think the evidence that there is a God is very minimal. He may think there is very little evidence that a certain religious way promotes the relationship with God. He may even regard several alternative conceptions of God not only as conceptually plausible but as live possibilities. He may regard certain alternative religious ways not only as plausible but also as having some probability of success. However, as long as he considers the value of attaining the good relationship with God to be qualitatively superior to any competing goals, and, as long as he believes a certain religious way has a better chance of attaining that end, the option of following that religious way will have a higher expected value than any other option. Thus, an expected value assessment yields that it is more rationally defensible for him to follow that religious way rather than not to do so. Formally stated, the decision problem of this person may be represented as follows:

Option A: Follow the religious way.

Option B: Do not follow the religious way.

For argument's sake, assume this person believes that if he chooses Option A, the probability that he will attain the good relationship with God is *very low*. Perhaps this is because he finds the standard critiques of belief in God to be very persuasive; so he is very dubious that there is a God. Suppose he is also very dubious about the authenticity of revelation. Let us say he considers the probability on option A that he will attain the good relationship with God to be 1/100. Let G be the value of attaining the good relationship with God. For argument's sake, suppose he believes that if he fails to attain

G, then his choice of Option A will result *in no value whatsoever*. Given these beliefs, the expected value of Option A is:

$$(1/100 \times G) + (99/100 \times 0) = G/100.$$

On the other hand, suppose he believes that on Option B there is a definite or 1/1 probability that he will attain some goal that has value *V*. We may imagine *V* to be very large; yet, by hypothesis, *G* is *qualitatively superior* to *V*. By hypothesis, such a person regards the probability that he will attain the good relationship with God to be *lower* if he chooses Option B rather than A. The reason is that, as explained in the previous section (3.6), the non-religious way is not plausible as a route to the good relationship with God. But let us allow that this person believes there is some very small probability that no matter how he acts, there is still some small probability that will result in his attaining *G* (in addition to attaining *V*). Suppose he considers the probability that he will attain *G* on option B to be 1/200. In this case, the expected value of Option B is:

$$1/1 \times V + 1/200 \times G = V + G/200.$$

Given these results, it follows that Option A will have a higher expected value than Option B if and only if:

$$G/100 > V + G/200.$$

Solving for *G*, this means that Option A will have the higher expected value if and only if:

$$G > 200 \times V.$$

Now, by hypothesis, *G* is supremely valuable, that is, qualitatively superior to any other goal. So, *G* is far more valuable than *V*, and indeed it is more valuable than $200 \times V$. Indeed, no matter what value *V* is multiplied by, *G* will always be more valuable than that product. Hence, the expected value of Option A is higher than that of Option B. Furthermore, we can now see that the specific probability assignments used above are immaterial to this outcome. *As long as the person conceives of G as qualitatively superior to V, and as long as he believes it is (even slightly) more probable that he will maintain or attain G by choosing Option A, then Option A will have a higher expected value than Option B*. Finally, since the calculation of this expected value is based on rationally defensible conceptions and beliefs, it follows that Option A is more rationally defensible than Option B.

It may be objected that even if the argument is technically sound, it seems odd or bizarre to make a decision about whether to be religious based on the application of a formula. Is this how people work, or should work, in real life? Do people, or should people, make religious decisions based on such calculations?

In response, philosophers often construct complex arguments on behalf of positions that many ordinary persons subscribe to, even if such persons never have and never will follow those complex arguments. No doubt it is true that most religious persons never have and never will consciously apply the Expected Value Principle to the case of religion. Nevertheless, the argument above may be taken as a refined articulation of a process that may go on beneath the surface for many, if not all, religious persons. The nub of the argument is that *it makes sense for someone to pursue what he conceives to be an uncertain but very great value, even at the risk of losing a certain but lesser value.* The rest of the argument is a refined articulation of that basic insight. The fact that many ordinary persons are not likely to be aware of the details of the argument is not a cogent objection to its validity. Their choice of a religious way may be rationally defensible in the way described above, even if they themselves cannot articulate that rationale.[84]

Advantages of the Present Argument over Pascal's Wager

The remainder of this section seeks to show that several standard objections raised against Pascal's Wager do not apply to this argument. (The reader may wish to reread the discussion of Pascal's Wager in Section 1.2.) Again, whether Pascal could have found some way to answer these objections is not our concern. In the process, the argument given here will become clearer.

The first objection considered above was that Pascal errs when he claims that the decision to believe in God or not is "forced." But, unlike Pascal's argument, the present argument does not seek to justify a *belief* using the pragmatic method. To the extent that a minimal belief in God is necessary for being a religious person, the argument above (in Section 3.5) uses *epistemic* or *evidential* means to support that belief. Furthermore, one *is* forced to choose whether or not to be religious. Failing to be religious is making a choice. It is impossible to be on the fence in this regard. Also, the objection about the moral and intellectual feasibility of inculcating a belief in oneself also does not apply to this argument. For this argument does not recommend pursuit of a belief in God *per se*. Rather it recommends the pursuit of a good relationship with God, even in the face of uncertainty whether God exists. This does not entail anything morally or intellectually infeasible. It is commonplace that people pursue all sorts of goals under conditions of uncertainty or even grave doubt about whether they will succeed. If the goal is deemed valuable enough, such a pursuit may not only be morally and intellectually permissible, but noble and admirable as well.

The second objection was that Pascal's Wager endorses an ignoble or even impious policy of pursuing a relationship with God solely out of a desire for self-interest or self-gain. This does not hold against the argument above. A person who makes the decision to pursue a good relationship with God based on considerations of value need not be focusing solely on his own self-interest. There are at least two reasons for this. First, as stated, the good relationship with God need not be conceived as a solitary matter between a private individual and God, but rather as part and parcel of a communal project. The person who pursues this relationship need not have only his own welfare in mind. Rather, he is seeking to be part of a good that is greater than himself. Second, whereas Pascal's Wager focuses on the attainment of "bliss" or "happiness," recall that the religious person conceives of the good relationship with God as both subjectively and objectively valuable. Thus, a person who pursues a good relationship with God may be trying to maximize his potential not only for attaining spiritual bliss or joy, but also for attaining a condition that he conceives to be *objectively* qualitatively superior to any other available state. In short, the use of an expected value calculation is not confined to cases of narrow self-interest.[85]

It is worth emphasizing that insofar as the argument of this book is pragmatic, the focus is on the potential value to be attained *from the relationship with God*. That relationship is understood in such a way that if one has that relationship, it permeates one's life and affects one's relationships with others as well. However, the argument above does *not* take into consideration any value that the religious life may have *independently* of whether it turns out that there is no God. For example, the religious life may have moral and esthetic spillover effects, so to speak. Conceivably, being religious gives one a sense of purpose and direction in life that one might lack otherwise. It may even have psychological and physiological benefits to be a religious believer, *even if it turns out that there is no God*.[86] The argument of this book does not appeal to this sort of value. Rather, the focus is on the potential value of having a good relationship with God, should it turn out that there is a God.

The next objection concerned Pascal's assumption that one can attain infinite bliss only if one believes in God. No such assumption is made here. A belief in God is not assumed to be sufficient, or even necessary for attaining infinite bliss, if there is such a thing, in the next world. Rather we have argued it is conceptually plausible to think that a religious way of life is more suitable as a means to a certain supremely valuable relationship with God. We have also argued that it is rationally defensible to believe that the probability that one will attain a certain relationship with God is higher if one adopts a religious way of life rather than if one does not.

Furthermore, the critical value at stake in the argument (the value of the good relationship with God) is not conceived as *infinite*, but rather as *finite, yet qualitatively superior* to other goods. This means that an option that has a higher chance of success at obtaining that superior value will have a higher expected value than any option that has a lower chance of obtaining that value. Thus, as stated above, even if the person *admits* that there is some small chance of obtaining the good relationship with God by *not* choosing the religious path, it will still be more rationally defensible to choose the religious way than not to do so.

Here then is another advantage of the present argument over Pascal's Wager. As noted earlier, the *more well developed* are one's conceptions of God, the good relationship with God, and so on, the *more rationally defensible* it is for a person to have those conceptions. Since being a religious theist involves having those conceptions, it follows that the more well developed are one's religious conceptions, the more rationally defensible it is to be a religious theist. A similar point holds for one's beliefs about God's reality or existence and one's beliefs about the doctrines that underlie one's religious way. Since the value of attaining the good relationship with God is conceived as *finite*, a way of life that has a greater probability of obtaining it will have a higher expected value than any alternative way of life. The more one can substantiate evidentially a belief in God, the higher will be the expected value of being a religious theist. If it could be shown (somehow) that it is rationally defensible to believe in God more confidently, then the expected value of following a religious way will increase. The expected value of following a certain religious way will be a product of the rationality of one's belief in God, together with the value considered to be at stake in successfully having the relationship with God.

The final objection we had considered against Pascal's Wager is known as the problem of "other gods." Pascal does not seem to recognize that some competing version of theistic belief might just as easily offer the same infinite reward in the next world. In which case, why would it be more rational to choose one version of theism than another? Perhaps the best thing to do under the circumstances is to hedge one's bets by remaining a non-believer, and hope that if there is a God at all, he will be all-forgiving. For the argument given above, one might pose an analogous objection, which might be called, the problem of "other religions." Suppose I am faced with two alternative religions, each of which invokes some tradition of revelation that recommends doing very different (and sometimes, mutually exclusive) things in order to attain a good relationship with God. Why would it be more rationally defensible to choose one religious way than the other? Under such circumstances, perhaps the wisest choice is not to be religious at all.

It is necessary to postpone a more complete response to this problem to Section 4.8, which deals with the issue of competing religions, and the prospect that there might be competing rationales for those different religions. However, some remarks are in place here.

There is no denying that, under certain circumstances, a person may indeed be in a situation where two competing religious ways turn out to be *equally* rationally defensible *for him*. However, it is important to note that, as a general rule, any two mutually exclusive or contradictory religious ways will involve two *different* conceptions of God and/or two *different* conceptions of the good relationship with God. Competing religions tend to offer not just alternative ways of getting *to* the same end, but rather, a somewhat different (and in some cases vastly different) conception *of* the end. Hence, the question of whether it is rational to choose or maintain one religious way as opposed to the other will depend (partly) on what particular conception of the end a person happens to have (so long as it meets the conditions for conceptual plausibility). When faced with two competing religious ways, the rational choice for a person will depend on how he or she answers the following questions: *What is my conception of God? What is my conception of the good relationship with God? Am I satisfied that my conceptions of God, the good relationship with God, and the religious way are plausible?* If the person has these conceptions and is satisfied that they are plausible, there is no reason for him to be concerned with the fact that on some *other* conception of God or the good relationship with God, a *different* religious way may be more appropriate.

An analogy is helpful here. Suppose I have a certain conception of what marriage should be like. It would be natural for me to have a certain accompanying conception of the type of person who would fit this conception of marriage. Suppose I also have some evidence for thinking that a certain person I have met fits the bill. Now, I might very well know that other people have a different conception of marriage. I might admit that *if* I had a different conception of marriage, a different person would better fit the bill. I might even admit that the alternative conception is just as coherent as mine, logically speaking. Under these circumstances, it will still be rationally defensible to court that person as a potential spouse, even though I admit that there are other equally coherent conceptions of marriage under which a different person would be a more suitable spouse. Similarly, if I am satisfied with my religious conceptions of God, the good relationship, and the religious way, it may still be rationally defensible to pursue that religious way even though I may admit that other conceptions are also plausible.[87]

However, suppose a person *does* happen to find two competing conceptions of God or the good relationship with God not only equally coherent, but also *equally appealing*. Such a person is "torn" about how to conceive of God or the good relationship with God. Still, it is possible that such a person might resolve his dilemma if he finds that the evidence for the doctrines underlying one religious way is better than the evidence for doctrines underlying the other religious way.[88] If he is capable of making this judgment, it will be rationally defensible for him to choose the one religious way over the other. It may happen (in fact, it does happen in the real world) that a person comes to find the conception of God, the good relationship, and so on, which he is familiar with to be implausible or in some way inferior to some competing conception. Or, he may come to determine that the evidence supporting the doctrines of some competing religious way is better than the evidence for that of his own religious way. If so, it will be rationally defensible for him to change religions. But this is not an *objection* to the argument above. It is rather a *desirable consequence* of that argument. So much on the problem of "other religions," at least for now.

We have argued that, so long as certain constraints are fulfilled, it is rationally defensible to be a religious theist. We have focused on the rational defensibility of religious theism in general, and left open whether some particular theistic religion, such as, for example, Judaism, Christianity, or Islam, can be shown to be rationally defensible. The only way to advance the argument further is to consider a specific version of religious theism and to ask whether it is rational to be a religious theist of that particular sort. This task is taken up in the next chapter, with Judaism as our example. Having done so, we shall then revisit the problem of "other religions."

Notes

1   See discussion above, Section 2.2.
2   The aim of this section is to articulate a concept of God that is common to the major theistic religions. Where appropriate, notes in this part refer to both Jewish and non-Jewish sources.
3   See discussion of this below, Section 3.7.
4   On the notion of God as supreme, see, for example, Isaiah 40:18–26 and Jeremiah 10:12–16. In the Koran, see 12.39, 14.48, and 87. The notion of God as in some sense a *person* or rational agent is implicit throughout the Jewish, Christian, and Islamic traditions. Perhaps the earliest and most direct biblical source for the notion that God is in some sense a person is the passage which states that God created the human "in his own image" (Genesis 1:27). This implies a similarity between God and the human person. For one recent discussion of the notion of God's personhood from a Christian perspective see Stanley Rudman, *Concepts of Person and Christian Ethics* (Cambridge: Cambridge University Press, 1997). In the Hindu tradition, the notion of God as Supreme Person is developed by, for example, Ramanuja (11th century). See the selection from his *Vedartha Samgraha* in *A Sourcebook in Asian Philosophy*, J.M. Koller and P. Koller, eds (New York: Macmillan, 1991) pp. 115–28. Regarding divergent tendencies (some towards monism and some towards theism) in early Hindu texts, see R.C. Zaehner's discussion in Chapter 4 ("God") in his book, *Hinduism* (Oxford: Oxford University Press, 1962).
5   The question of whether God "really" has qualities or properties is a vexed issue. Those who adopt "negative theology" claim that in the final analysis, God does not really have any properties or qualities. Yet, even such philosophers agree that at some level of discourse, we may (and sometimes must) speak *as if* God has certain properties. This is certainly the case for negative theologians who are committed to any of the major versions of religious theism including Judaism, Christianity, Islam and theistic Hinduism. Hence, whether or not God really has properties, we can still ask whether there is any reason for conceiving of God *as if* he has certain properties rather than others. How those ascriptions of properties to God are to be understood in the final analysis remains an open question, which we do not need to enter in this book. This book does not endorse, nor deny, the viability of the "negative way." However, the discussion below about God's "ontological category" may bear on this debate.
6   For a concise discussion of such arguments, see William J. Wainwright, *Philosophy of Religion* (Belmont: Wadsworth, 1988) pp. 6–10.
7   This follows in the tradition of Anselm's famous description of God as "that than which none greater can be conceived" (*Proslogium* II). However, it also introduces the idea

that God is the best *kind* of being. Incidentally, my use of the disjunctive phrase "being or reality" is not redundant; it is intentionally vague on whether God is conceived as a being who exists, or some other sort of reality. See the discussion below on God's "ontological category."

8   See below, Section 3.7.

9   See Charles Hartshorne, *The Logic of Perfection* (LaSalle, Ontario: Open Court, 1962) and *A Natural Theology for Our Time* (LaSalle, Ontario: Open Court, 1967).

10 On whether God has properties at all, see note 5 above.

11 See Moses Maimonides, *Code of Jewish Law*: Fundamentals of the Torah 1:1–3. For one recent discussion of God's attributes, see Wainwright, *Philosophy of Religion*, Chapter 1, and the select bibliography on p. 30. For another bibliography, see M. Peterson et. al., eds., *Philosophy of Religion: Selected Readings* (Oxford: Oxford University Press, 2001) p. 161.

12 Does oneness or uniqueness somehow follow logically from the other traits? It seems we could conceive the possibility that there be *many* essentially necessary and independent realities. See discussion later on this point, in the discussion of God's "ontological category."

13 If this view is correct, it would seem that with respect to his value commitments, the religious theist's position is *rationally permissible*, if not *rationally defensible*. On rational permissibility, see Chapter 1, note 6.

14 For a collection of essays on this notion, see Scott MacDonald, ed., *Being and Goodness: the concept of the good in metaphysics and philosophical theology* (Ithaca: Cornell University Press, 1991).

15 *Nicomachean Ethics*, Bk. I: vii.

16 It might be objected that this way of putting the question seems to presuppose some version of "essentialism" or "doctrine of natural kinds", that is, the view that everything has a certain essence or nature which is "what it really is." In truth, many theists accept such a doctrine, since they think that God created the world and endowed things with "natures." However, this objection is not on the mark here. Skepticism about whether there is such a thing as a natural kind may very well apply to Aristotle's claim that we can evaluate how good something is insofar as it is a being *of a certain natural or essential kind.* Thus for example, Aristotle claims that the human has a certain nature or "natural function." But the claim here is that we can formulate the question, *is x good insofar as its being is concerned?* This question suggests that there is some way of evaluating whether some beings are better than others. But it does not presuppose a natural kinds doctrine.

17 It has also been argued on these very same grounds that immutability and impassibility should be ascribed to God. Change and mutability seem like a "defect" in one's being (see Wainwright, *Philosophy of Religion*, p. 13 and pp. 15–19). We shall consider this issue later.

18 There are different ways of trying to understand this in more detail, depending on one's theory of causation or explanation. Descartes in the *Meditations* (see Meditation 3) seems to understand causation in a rather "hydraulic" fashion, such that for one being to cause another being is for the first being to "transfer" some of its own being or reality to the second. If this is correct, then a being that can cause or sustain all other beings must have sufficient reality or being to pull this off. It must have more being or reality than all else put together. However, in order to establish the relevant point, the argument in the main text here does not rely on this or any other particular theory of causation or explanation. Many will agree that, for example, the greatness of an artwork is a reflection or sign of a greatness within the artist. An artist who can produce greater artwork is greater *as an artist* than one who can produce only lesser art. Saying this does not require any particular theory about how causation works, certainly not one that involves transfer of reality or being (from artist to artwork). Similarly, without any

particular theory of causation or explanation in hand, it still makes sense to think of a being or reality that can cause or ground all else as one that is superior to all else.

19 See, for example, R. Swinburne, *The Coherence of Theism* (Oxford: Clarendon Press, 1986). See, for example, pp. 98–99 where Swinburne characterizes theism as the claim that "there exists eternally an omnipresent spirit, free, creator of the universe, omnipotent, omniscient, perfectly good, and a source of moral obligation ... ."

20 See Maimonides, *Guide to the Perplexed*, I:54.

21 Again, there is also a debate about whether the attributes (both the necessary and contingent ones) "really inhere" or "really do not inhere" in God's essence. This relates to the debate about negative theology, already mentioned above. Those inclined toward a more "simple" divine essence will argue against attributes inhering in God; those inclined toward a "richer" divine essence might argue for such attributes. Those inclined toward the former might say that "wisdom," "benevolence", and "justice" are not separate properties that really inhere in God's essence; rather it is the case that God's essence is utterly "simple" and that we ascribe these terms to God only to characterize God's actions. It is not necessary to enter this debate here. However, see below, note 30.

22 For one attempt to work out a contemporary metaphysics that is not avowedly theistic, but is in some respects sympathetic to the conception of God presented here, see *The Faces of Existence: an essay in non-reductive metaphysics*, by John F. Post (Ithaca: Cornell University Press, 1987) especially Chapter 8 ("God").

23 For a survey of several significant philosophers whose metaphysical views tend to favor this approach, see *In Search of Deity: an essay in Dialectical Theism* by John Macquarrie, especially "Part Two: Representatives of an Alternative Tradition" (New York: Crossroad, 1985). Macquarrie discusses, among others, Plotinus, John Scotus Eriugena, Hegel, and Heidegger. However, as Macquarrie recognizes, not all of these thinkers are properly characterized as theists (particularly Heidegger). The contrast Macquarrie sets up between Classical Theism and what he calls Dialectical Theism is not identical to the contrast set up here between what I have called the "standard" and "alternative" conceptions of God. A full discussion of the differences between the present conception and Macquarrie's conception (and other non-standard conceptions) must be reserved for another occasion.

24 Some philosophers (for example, Platonists) claim that there are *abstract* entities, such as redness, triangularity, equality, and so on. On this view, Redness is an entity that exists. There is no need to enter this dispute here. Even if there is such an entity as Redness, this is certainly a very different kind of entity than an entity that is a concrete, particular red thing.

25 Again, some philosophers (Platonists) may claim precisely that there is such a thing as the entity, Being. Whether or not this is so, sentence E is still true.

26 Something similar could be done with the concept of Truth: *Every true proposition exhibits Truth.* If we followed this latter route, we could articulate the concept of God's essence as *Truth* (rather than as *Being*). That is an alternative not explored here.

27 In Hebrew, the term *Havayah* sometimes means "being" in the abstract sense and sometimes means "a being." This term is etymologically related to the Tetragrammaton (the proper name of God in the Hebrew Scriptures).

28 Unless, of course, one adopts the (Platonist) view that Being is an entity, which exists.

29 There is a philosophical debate about the status of necessary truths. Do they say something about the world or rather about the way we think or about the way we use words? Are all necessary truths "trivial"? Also, there is a debate about how we *know* necessary truths. Do we have some special power to intuit or grasp necessary truths? Is it an empirical discovery? Is it a matter of *language* that necessary truths are true? These are debates we need not enter. No matter what view one takes on these questions, one can still view God's essence as Being and regard *necessity* as a feature of Being.

30 One may ask, are the features of necessity, independence, and so on features which

"inhere" in Being? We may avoid taking a stance on this, just as we did earlier on the debate over negative theology. Whether the negative theologian would prefer to speak of "features that inhere in Being" rather than "properties that inhere in *a being*" is another matter. It depends on what is the motivation for endorsing negative theology in the first place. It might turn out that this alternative conception of God's ontological category has certain affinities with those who adopt the standard conception of God but endorse negative theology. But this is not an issue we need pursue here.

31   There is a philosophical dispute on whether principles or laws are themselves entities – but this is a dispute we need not enter in order to set up the contrast between the standard and the alternative conceptions of God.

32   A different alternative would be to conceive of God as a series of principles, perhaps with a fundamental single underlying principle as God's essence. Another alternative would be to say that God has *no* essence, and that all we need to do to articulate the concept of God is to articulate the divine principles. Another alternative (alluded to in note 26 above) is to conceive of God's essence as Truth (rather than as Being).

33   Religious philosophers differ on the question of whether the move to positing such divine principles is rationally justifiable or not. An advocate of a teleological-style argument for belief in God would claim that such a move is justifiable. He would argue that the only way to adequately explain scientific laws themselves is to posit some theistic or divine principles. This type of argument is neither endorsed nor rejected here.

34   Some theists may hold that there are some things, which even God cannot know. See note 43 below on divine foreknowledge.

35   This brings up the debate between libertarianism and soft-determinism. The soft-determinist would say that God's action is free so long as it is neither random nor constrained by some external force. But it may be necessitated by something within God's essence. On the libertarian conception of freedom, one must add that God's action is free if it is neither random, nor constrained by any external *nor internal* force or necessity.

36   An issue we need not enter is to what extent does God set up an order that operates on its own, and to what extent does God intervene in the way the world works? This relates to the issue of miracles. See note 40 below.

37   However, one can always press the question, *why did (or does) God choose to express himself?* The soft-determinist might say that this choice flowed from God's nature necessarily. For the libertarian, such a view compromises God's freedom. On the libertarian account, the best the theist can do is to say that given the kind of being that God is, God's choice to express himself *makes sense*, even though it is not necessitated thereby.

38   Again, there may be some true facts, which even God does not know. See the discussion below on divine foreknowledge.

39   However, as suggested later, the divine principles may themselves be explained in light of the necessary features (metaphysical attributes) of being.

40   Issues analogous to certain matters of debate mentioned in connection with the standard conception also arise here. For example, what is the precise relationship between the divine principles and scientific laws? Is there ever a case when a scientific law is *overridden* by a divine principle? If so, that would constitute a miracle.

41   The libertarian vs. soft-determinism debate will be reiterated in a different form here. The libertarian will say the divine principles, or at least some of them, are not necessary, but are *explicable* by appeal to certain features of Being. The soft-determinist will say that the divine principles are, in principle, *completely* explicable given the necessary features of Being.

42   This is the view of, for example, Sankara (8th century). For a discussion of Sankara's views see Wainwright, *Philosophy of Religion*, pp. 10–12 and *Asian Philosophies*, J.M. Koller and P. Koller, eds (New Jersey: Prentice Hall, 1998) pp. 74–80.

43   There is also an objection dealing with God's knowledge, which could be dealt with in

a similar way. The objection is that if God knows the world, then whenever the world changes, God changes too. The standard conception can respond by admitting there is some kind of change in God due to the changing of his knowledge, but this is not essential change. Or, it can say that, somehow, God knows the future from time immemorial, so in effect he doesn't change. This brings up the issue of divine foreknowledge of future contingents (see note 44). The alternative conception says that God's knowledge of the world has to do with the fact that the world has a certain structure. That *structure* does not change, even if *events* within the world constantly are changing. This is just like saying, the law of gravity does not change, even though physical objects governed by this law are constantly undergoing change in position.

44   To date, it seems no philosopher has convincingly shown that it is logically impossible for God to have certain foreknowledge of future contingents. But suppose it did turn out, that it is logically impossible for some being or reality to know future contingents. In this case, the theist will have to admit that God doesn't have such knowledge. However, even if this is so, the theist can still maintain the conception of God as qualitatively superior to any other *logically possible* kind of being or reality. Incidentally, on the alternative conception, what might it mean to say that God knows some future free act? Roughly, it means that the world is organized or structured in such a way that there are certain things happening right now because of a) certain divine principles (such as benevolence, justice, and so on) together with the fact that b) some future free act will occur. For example, consider the statement, "God knows that tomorrow Alex will freely choose to go on a shooting spree at the mall." On the alternative conception, this means that the world is structured in such a way that, for example, John who works at the mall may fall ill and not be able to go to work tomorrow, precisely because of a) certain divine principles (benevolence, justice, and so on) together with the fact that b) Alex will choose to go on a shooting spree. Other particular facts may also be relevant here, such as perhaps the fact that it is part of the divine plan that John is not yet destined to die. In other words, the doctrine of divine foreknowledge comes down to the doctrine that some present events are in part to be explained by that fact that certain future events will occur. This is known as "backward causation" or "backward explanation." Whether this is logically possible or not is an issue we cannot explore here.

45   See the discussion of the religious way, below, Section 3.4.

46   This point seems harder to make on the libertarian position but it can be done. The libertarian would argue that if x necessitated y due to x's *internal* properties or features, x couldn't help itself so to speak; x was fated to do what it did. Hence, x is not as genuine a cause of y as it would be if it were not internally constrained to do so.

47   This argument works regardless of whether God is conceived as *a being* or as *Being*. If God is conceived as *a being*, the idea is that a being which is a free cause is metaphysically superior to a being which is not, because only the former genuinely contains within itself the wherewithal to cause its effect. On the other hand, if God is conceived as Being, the idea is that one can conceive of Being as either a non-free ground (that is, explanation) of all things, or as a free ground. If Being is not free, then, it does not genuinely "ground" anything else. Either there is no real grounding (that is, explanation) here at all, or, the real explanation for why it "grounds" all else lies outside itself. In either case, it would not be metaphysically supreme. If it genuinely contains within itself the wherewithal to ground (explain) all other beings, then it must be free. As a clarification, it must be emphasized that the present argument does *not* assert that there is a ground or cause of all things, nor does it insist that if there is a ground or cause of all things, then it *must* be free. Rather, the argument insists that *if* there is a ground or cause of all things, and *if* that ground or cause is *supreme*, then it is free.

48   Incidentally, this is one way of interpreting the scriptural passage, which says that the human is created in the image of God. To say this is to say that, like God, human beings have freedom. This is what makes them divine, in a certain sense. At the same time,

human freedom is only an "image" of divine freedom. See the commentaries of Ovadiah Seforno and Meir Simcha of Dvinsk to Genesis 1:26. Their interpretations are quoted in *Sefer Bereshit with commentary Daat Mikra* by Yehuda Kil (Jerusalem: Mossad Harav Kook, 1997) p. 26.

49   Some philosophers (for example, Kant) think that *only* persons have intrinsic worth. This view is not endorsed here. Others might allow that some non-persons (even trees?) have intrinsic worth. This is a debate we need not enter. Incidentally, infants may require separate discussion. They can be treated as more valuable than non-persons because they are potential persons or because they are already valued especially by persons or because pragmatically it is impossible to tell when an infant crosses the line into personhood, or for several other reasons.

50   The notion of God as morally supreme is found, for example, in Deuteronomy, 32:4; Psalms 145:17; Koran 1:1–3. In the Hindu tradition, see Ramanuja's description of the Supreme Person in Koller and Koller, *Asian Philosophies*, p. 128.

51   This raises the question of whether God must create the best of all possible worlds, and similar conundrums. It also raises the "problem of evil." For a discussion of this problem see Wainwright, *Philosophy of Religion*, Chapter 3. Of course, whether it is in fact *true* that a morally supreme God exists is a separate issue. Here we are just talking about the *concept* of God.

52   This point would have to be refined if God's intellectual supremacy is not understood in terms of omniscience. See discussion above, note 44.

53   See Wainwright, *Philosophy of Religion*, pp. 13–15.

54   This is a classic idea found in many traditional sources. See Moshe Hayyim Luzzatto (1707–47), *The Way of God* (New York: Feldheim, 1978) Part I: Chapter 2: Section 1 (p. 37).

55   See ibid.

56   This idea is based on Moshe Hayyim Luzzatto's rationale for why God created people with freedom. See *The Way of God*, Part I: Chapter 2: Section 2 (p. 39) and I:3:1 (p. 45). Luzzatto says that God is essentially good. This is the best way a being can be good. Now, God seeks to share his goodness with others. Since he is the best, he also wishes to share his goodness so that others have it in the best possible way. Yet God is faced with a logical constraint: he cannot share essential goodness with anything that is dependent! God's solution is to create a mechanism whereby dependent creatures can "merit" or earn their goodness. In this way, they mimic the way in which God has his goodness. In short, the creation of beings with freedom and responsibility and the potential for righteousness (and consequently wickedness) is a means of divine self-expression.

57   Nothing in either the standard or alternative conception of God's ontological status itself determines whether God is provident in a general or particular way. If God is conceived along the lines of the alternative conception, it does not follow that particular providence is ruled out. One could just as easily conceive of God as a being with properties, and regard God as interested in the world only in a very general manner. Conversely, one may conceive of the divine secondary attributes as principles which describe the order and structure of the world, and still think that those principles are very "fine grained," such that depending on how human beings act in very particular ways in very particular situations, different things will occur.

58   Roots of this view are found in Plotinus, *Enneads*, VI:9:11. Cf. Dionysus the Areopagite, *Mystical Theology*, Chapter 1. See also Sermon 5 in *Meister Eckhart: A Modern Translation* (London: Harper, 1941) and Sermon XXII in *Meister Eckhart: An Introduction to the Study of His Works with an Anthology of his Sermons* (New York: Nelson, 1957). However, the issue of whether Eckhart maintains that ultimately there remains some unbridgeable gap between God and creatures is a vexed one. See Clarke's discussion in ibid., p. 90. See also Catherine of Genoa, *Purgation and Purgatory and the Spiritual Dialogue* (New York: Paulist Press, 1979) p. 80 and p. 86.

59   On the motivation for the project of formulating a rational defense for being religious, see above Section 1.3.

60   The notion that God has some special good in store for the righteous is expressed in Psalms 27:13 and 31:19. Rabbinic sources interpret these passages as hinting at a reward in the world to come (see *Midrash Tehillim* ad. loc.). Reward in a hereafter is explicitly referred to in the New Testament (see John 3:16 and Romans 2:7 and in the Koran, 3.148 8.67 9.38, 10.64.

61   See above, Section 1.2.

62   It seems the following is a response Pascal could have made as well. But this is a matter of interpretation we need not enter.

63   For another way in which a relationship with God could be conceived as "objectively valuable," see below, Section 4.3.

64   In describing the relationship between God and Israel, the Hebrew Scriptures invoke the relationship between father and son (Exodus 4:22); king and servant (Ezekiel 20:33); husband and wife (Hosea 2:18). On the notion of forming a bond (*devekut*) with God in the Hebrew Scriptures, see Deuteronomy 10:20. On love of God, see Deuteronomy 6:5 and 10:12. More detail on the Jewish notion *devekut* follows below (Chapter 17). On love of God in the Christian scriptures, see Matthew 22:37; Mark 12:30; John 15: 9–10. For love of God in Hinduism see the Bhagavad Gita 6:31, 8:14, 8:22, 9:33–34, 18: 55–57. For medieval discussions of love of God see Moses Maimonides, *Guide for the Perplexed*, III:51 and Aquinas, *Summa Theologiae*, 1a:43:3. See also John of the Cross, *The Ascent of Mount Carmel*, II:5. For more recent discussions, in the Jewish tradition, see Schneur Zalman of Liadi, *Tanya* (Brooklyn. Kehot Publication Society, 1968–69) especially chapters 41–44. Cf. Martin Buber, *I and Thou* (New York: Scribner, 2000). In the Christian tradition, see John Cowburn, *The Person and Love: Philosophy and Theology of Love* (Norwitch: Fletcher & Sons Ltd., 1967) and Vincent Brummer, *The Model of Love*. In the Hindu tradition, see M. Dhavamony, *Love of God according to Saiva Siddhanta: A study in the Mysticism and Theology of Saivism* (Oxford: Clarendon Press, 1971) and Jadunath Sinha, *Jivagosvami's Religion of Devotion and Love* (Varnasi: Chowkhamba Vidyabhawan, 1983). For a discussion of the attempt to bond or unite with God in Islam, see Jean-Louis Michon, "The Spiritual Practices of Sufism" in *Islamic Spirituality: Foundations*, ed. S.H. Nasr (New York: Crossroads, 1997) pp. 265–93. See also the discussion of Ibn Sina and Sufism in *Asian Philosophies*, pp. 97–100. For reverence or fear of God in Jewish sources, see Deuteronomy 6:13, 24; 8:6. See also Maimonides, *Code of Jewish Law*, Fundamentals of the Torah, II:1, 2. On reverence of God generally, see the classic work by Rudolf Otto, *The Idea of the Holy* (New York: Oxford University Press, 1958).

65   On this point, see John of the Cross, *Ascent of Mount Carmel*, II:5; Cowburn, *The Person and Love*, pp. 347–55; Brummer, *The Model of Love* pp. 214–23.

66   On this view, as long as something has intrinsic worth or value, it is due at least some measure of respect. Whether non-persons have intrinsic value is a debatable question. Earlier a rationale was presented for thinking that persons have greater intrinsic value than non-persons; but that does not rule out the possibility that non-persons (for example, animals, trees, the environment) might have some intrinsic value.

67   It is not necessary here to enter a detailed account of awe or reverence. For a general discussion see Otto, *The Idea of the Holy*.

68   What is the relation between respect for God and respect for other persons? A full discussion of this is not necessary for the present purpose. However, the following seems plausible. Respect for *x* involves the recognition of the worth or value of *x*, insofar as *x* is a certain kind of being or thing. Arguably, recognition and appreciation of the worth or value of *x* requires the willingness to recognize and appreciate intrinsic worth or value *wherever* it is found. Thus, in order to genuinely respect God, one must respect anyone or anything that has intrinsic worth or value. On the other hand, it is

plausible to think that one's respect for God should be much deeper than one's respect for any human person. Respect should be proportionate to the value of the object or person respected. Thus, respect for God involves the attitudes of dread, awe, reverence and a disposition to worship and obedience. Such attitudes would be inappropriate to direct toward any thing or being other than God.

69   There may be some sense in which God can be said to "love" even those who willfully spurn God's way; but that is a different sense of love. There is surely some sense in which God loves the "righteous" and does *not* love the wicked. In the Hebrew Scriptures, God is depicted as *hating* the wicked. See for example, Psalms 5:6.

70   This is one way of interpreting what is meant by God's statement, "I will dwell among them" (Exodus 25:8 and 29:45). God "dwells among" the community of religious persons by imbuing the community with the divine character.

71   What is the relationship between love of God and love of others? A full discussion of this is not necessary for the present purpose. However, the following seems plausible. Love involves the effort to form a bond with some particular thing or being or person precisely insofar as there is something intrinsically valuable or worthwhile about *that* particular being or thing. As stated earlier (note 68) the recognition and appreciation of something as intrinsically valuable requires a willingness or disposition to recognize and appreciate value or worth *wherever* it is found. However, we have also argued that love of a particular someone requires *particular knowledge* of that someone. So one can't in this sense "love everyone." (There might be some *other* legitimate sense of the term "love" in which one could.) Therefore, in contradistinction to what we said about respect, love of God does not *require* love for one's self, nor for any particular others. But, arguably, love of God does require a *disposition* to love oneself and others, which under most normal circumstances will be fulfilled or should be fulfilled at least to some degree. A person who loves God for his character traits should be disposed, *mutatis mutandis*, to love other persons who have intrinsically valuable or worthy character traits as well. All the same, it seems plausible to think that love of any person or object should be proportionate to the intrinsic value or worth of that person or object. Hence one's love for God should be qualitatively different from one's love for any being or thing other than God.

72   There is a vast literature on the notions of contemplation and meditation. For one approach, see Thomas Merton, *What is contemplation?* (London: Burns, Oates and Washbourne, 1950). See also Aryeh Kaplan, *Jewish Meditation* (New York: Schocken Books, 1995).

73   How far can those practices go in not making sense to us without straining the limits of conceptual plausibility is a controversial question. See discussion of this below (Section 4.4).

74   See Section 2.3, p. 23.

75   Some may find the *a priori* style of argument such as the Ontological Argument for God's existence more persuasive than the argument from religious experience. Others may find the more traditional arguments, for example, cosmological, teleological arguments, and so on more persuasive. If these arguments have any merit, that only helps the case here. Yet without some version of the argument from religious experience, it seems that one will not have even minimal evidence for the existence or reality of God *as a person who has engaged in communication with humans*. Hence, the argument from religious experience turns out to be crucial for theistic commitment in a way that the other arguments are not.

76   See for example, R. Swinburne, *The Existence of God* (Oxford: Clarendon Press, 1979) pp. 244–76.

77   See Wainwright, *Philosophy of Religion*, Chapter 3, especially pp. 69–72.

78   We may distinguish several types of atheists. One type *admits* there is some evidence for God, but happens not to believe in God. Another type happens to be in the position of

believing that there is no live possibility that God exists. But he does not have a view on whether his belief is rationally defensible. Another type believes there is no live possibility that God exists, and thinks that his view is rationally defensible. But he admits that others (for example, those having religious experiences) may have a rationally defensible belief in the live possibility (or even, high probability) of a God. Another type believes that the view that it is *very unlikely* that there is a God is not only rationally defensible, but also rationally compelling. Even such a person may grant there is a live possibility that there is a God. Finally, what we might call the "hard-core" atheist believes there is *no live possibility* that there is a God, *and* thinks his view is not only rationally defensible but also rationally compelling. It would seem that the group of hard-core atheists constitutes a relatively small proportion of all atheists.

79   However, see below, Section 3.7. The standard project is relevant to the project of this book in that the *more* well supported the belief in God is, the *more* rationally defensible it is to be religious.

80   See Section 2.3.

81   One could quibble with this assumption by imagining peculiar scenarios, in which the intelligent extraterrestrials might be the sort who make a decision to communicate with us only on condition that we *don't* communicate with them. They might be the type that gets scared off by our attempts. Or, they might wish to communicate with us only if we play "hard to get." But such extraterrestrials would not be "friendly." Anyway, such quibbles would not apply in the case of God, who is conceived as morally and intellectually supreme.

82   One might try to block this inference by posing the following scenario. Suppose we have no way of ruling out the possibility that some very powerful third party (human or alien) unbeknownst to us has the goal of interfering with our attempts to send out such communication. If so, we are *not* increasing the probability that we will communicate with the intelligent extraterrestrials by sending out signals. However, again, this scenario would not apply in the case of God, who is conceived as supremely powerful.

83   Note that the claim here is that conditions 1), 2), and 3) are *sufficient* conditions for having the belief in question. This leaves open that there may be *other* conditions under which it is rationally defensible to believe that engaging in the actions based on *R* increase the probability that one will attain the good relationship with God.

84   See the discussion about deference to authority in Section 2.2, p. 19.

85   In Pascal's defense, it is sometimes suggested that Pascal's intended target for his argument is someone who is avowedly self-interested. Perhaps Pascal could have made much the same response by altering the terms of his argument. Instead of talking about infinite *bliss* or *happiness*, he could have just as easily talked about infinite *goodness*.

86   William James considers mainly this kind of value in his essay, "The Will to Believe," in *Essays in Pragmatism* (New York: Hafner, 1955) pp. 88–109. There are many popular defenses of religious commitment based on "spillover" benefits of this sort. However, this approach seems vulnerable to the objection that it endorses a religious commitment that is not devout.

87   Compare William James' point about live options, in "The Will to Believe," p. 89.

88   Such a response seems unavailable to Pascal as a defense of the Wager against the problem of "other gods." Due to his use of infinite value, it appears that belief in any god that has any small chance of resulting in the infinite gain turns out to be just as pragmatically rational as belief in any other god.

Chapter 4

The Rationality of Being a Religious Jew[1]

4.1 General Remarks

In order to address the question at hand, we must develop some conception of what is involved in being a religious Jew. We had stated that a person is a religious theist if and only if he or she fulfills a certain set of conditions. That definition covers many if not most Christians, Muslims, Jews, some Hindus, and others as well. We may now tailor these conditions to cover *only* religious Jews in the following way. A person is a religious Jew if and only if:

1 He has a Jewish conception of God.
2 He has a Jewish conception of what constitutes a good relationship with God.
3 He has a Jewish conception of what constitutes the religious way, that is, the way to attain that relationship.
4 He believes there is (at least) a *live possibility* that there is a God (according to the Jewish conception).
5 He believes that it is (*at least slightly*) more likely that he will attain or maintain the good relationship with God if he follows the Jewish religious way than if he does not do so.
6 He follows the Jewish religious way.

This provides a basic framework for what is involved in being a religious Jew. However, we need to articulate further some of these conditions. It is not the aim here to work out the notion of the religious Jew in full detail, but only to articulate a conception that differentiates the religious Jew from other religious theists. In this part, we shall articulate the conditions for being a religious Jew, and also argue that, at least for some persons, it is rationally defensible to fulfill each and all of these conditions.

A word on the structure of this book may be helpful. Chapter 2 articulated the religious theist, and Chapter 3 described the conditions under which it is rationally defensible to be a religious theist. However, for the sake of brevity, this chapter articulates the religious Jew *and* describes the conditions under which it is rationally defensible to be one. The reader should bear in mind that these are two separate projects. Thus, for example, the reader might agree with the present articulation of the religious Jew, but disagree with the claim that it is rationally defensible to be one. Alternatively, the reader might quibble with the articulation of the religious Jew, but agree that given that articulation, it is rationally defensible to be one.

At the outset, something must be said about what counts as a *Jewish* conception. Any proposal to articulate the Jewish conceptions of God, the good relationship with God, and so on, should be well grounded in those texts which are widely acknowledged to be the classic Jewish sources, namely, the Hebrew Scriptures and the rabbinic literature (that is, the Talmud and Midrashic compilations). Of course, what counts as a "well-grounded" proposal may be a matter of interpretation and debate. I submit that the proposal offered below is well grounded in the classic Jewish sources. However, there is no claim here that this proposal is the *only* well-grounded one.[2]

4.2 The Jewish Conception of God: The Supreme Person

The first condition is that the person has a Jewish conception of God. While different Jewish theologians and philosophers may develop and extend the concept of God in different ways, the Jewish conception is basically the one articulated earlier, namely, God as *Supreme Person*. That notion is rooted in classic Jewish texts, including the Hebrew Scriptures and the rabbinic writings.[3] In contrast, a Christian for example might need or want to add certain features to the concept of God, such as the trinity. But the religious Jew does not need to add anything to the basic God-concept articulated earlier.

Saying this does not preclude that the religious Jew may be committed to (at least) a (minimal) belief that God does or has done certain other things, *beyond* what is implied by basic God-concept. Indeed, we shall see later (Condition 5) that the religious Jew is committed to (at least) a (minimal) belief that *God has chosen the people of Israel* and that *God has given the Torah to Israel*. However, these tenets do not follow *a priori* from the basic God-concept, and one does not need to view such additional doctrines as part and parcel of the very concept of God.

Some students of Judaism may be inclined to disagree with this approach. They might insist that a religious Jew is committed to conceiving of God "definitionally" as having certain other essential traits or properties not included in the basic God concept, such as, for example, that God is the "God of Abraham, Isaac, and Jacob." For that matter, one might be inclined to think of the Jewish God as essentially "God the Torah-giver or Lawgiver." However, there is a difficult question here about whether such features need to be viewed as part and parcel of the very concept of God or rather as ways of talking about what God does or has done according to Jewish teachings.[4]

For the present purpose, here we adopt the latter view. The Jewish conception of God *just is* the basic God-concept articulated already. This does not preclude the possibility that some Jewish theologians may want to argue that other features should be added to the basic God-concept. And, as already stated, it does not preclude that the religious Jew is committed to believing (at least minimally) certain additional doctrines about God's actions that are not implied by or included in the basic God-concept.

Now, we have already argued that the basic concept of God articulated in the previous part is conceptually plausible. On the view adopted here that the Jewish concept of God *just is* the basic God concept, it follows that the Jewish concept of God is conceptually plausible.

Before moving on, we must consider the following question. What is the religious Jew committed to regarding *non-Jewish* versions of the conception of God, such as, for example, a Christian conception? It is of course possible that the religious Jew may find that some given alternative conception of God is internally incoherent or implausible. However, this need not be the case. A religious Jew may have a conceptually plausible conception of God, and still admit that other variations on that concept are also plausible, that is, internally coherent. He may even admit that some *non*-theistic conception of ultimate reality or being is conceptually plausible. Of course, that's not how *he* conceives of God or ultimate reality. We shall return to this issue later.

4.3 The Jewish Conception of the Good Relationship with God: *Devekut*

The second condition for being a religious Jew is that the person must have a Jewish conception of the good relationship with God. In the previous chapter we discussed three different ways of how a religious theist might conceive the good relationship with God: 1) radical union with God, 2) attainment of some great good caused by God, and 3) interpersonal relationship with God. There is not too much in the Hebrew Scriptures or rabbinic literature which would support conception 1. There are also serious conceptual problems with this view, as discussed earlier in Chapter 3. Now, there seems to be ample support for conception 2, especially in the rabbinic writings. The Talmud teaches that there is a reward in the next world for the religious Jew.[5] One could easily view the good relationship with God as the attainment of this reward. However, the bulk of the classic Jewish sources supports conception 3.[6] That is, the goal of the religious Jew is to attain, maintain, and improve a certain kind of interpersonal relationship with God. We have already seen that this conception has certain theoretical advantages over conceptions 2 and 3. We shall adopt that conception here as well.[7]

On this view, the Jewish conception of the good relationship with God is that of a certain kind of interpersonal bond between the religious person and

God. Everything said in the previous part regarding that relationship, including the discussion of love and respect, is entirely consistent with Jewish sources. Nevertheless, one could have the conception of the good relationship with God as interpersonal bond and still *not* have a Jewish conception of the relationship. After all, the notion that love and respect of God is the best way of relating to God is found in many traditions aside from Judaism. For example, this notion is found in Christianity, Islam, as well as certain forms of Hinduism.[8]

In this section we shall elaborate the features that must be added in order to arrive at the particularly Jewish conception of that relationship. To do this, we must describe two fundamental teachings of the Jewish sources, which involve certain historical or factual claims made about what God does or has done in the past. These are the doctrine of the chosenness of the Jewish people and the doctrine that God has given the Torah to the Jewish people. It will emerge that the latter doctrine implies or presupposes the former doctrine. However, it is worth separating the two doctrines for purposes of exposition.

First, the doctrine of chosenness. The Hebrew Scriptures claim that God has established a certain relationship with the nation or people of Israel.[9] God has chosen the people of Israel as special, and it is especially with Israel that God seeks to form an interpersonal bond. God has formed a covenant or pact with Israel. Furthermore, the good relationship with God can blossom fully only in the context of a *community* of religious Jews. Thus, the term "interpersonal" should not be taken to denote a private relationship between God and each individual Jew, but rather a communal relationship between God and the community of Jews. Let us further articulate that communal relationship. We can then turn to the role of the individual within that context.

The major components of this relationship are mutual recognition/respect and mutual love between the community and God.[10] Everything said about love and respect in the previous part applies here, though with a more specifically Jewish twist. Our discussion in what follows is based on Jewish theological and philosophical literature.

Let us first discuss what constitutes the community's respect for God. Respect for God means not only having a cognitive awareness or knowledge of God's reality or existence, but also a certain attitudinal or emotional response to God, namely, the fear of and reverence for God. This involves a fear of the possibility of God's punishment if one violates God's will, but also a more elevated sort of attitude, namely, a reverence or respect for God, just for what God is – the Supreme Person. Reverence for God inspires a willingness to obey God's will, independently of the fear of God's punishment. Similarly, love for God also involves two aspects: a love of God for what God provides, and a more elevated sort of love of God just for what God is, the Supreme Person.[11] To love God is not only to appreciate and acknowledge the goodness of God, but also to obey and worship God.

Moreover, the love of God involves the effort to be spiritually intimate with God. We shall refer to this relationship using the Hebrew term, *devekut*, which means, "cleaving" or "bonding" with God.[12] This is the apex of the religious community's good relationship with God. To attain *devekut* with God is to establish a connection with the very personhood and/or personality of God. More on this notion shortly.

So far we have discussed the community's recognition and love of God. How does God express recognition for the Jewish community? Given their status as unequals, there is no place for God to "fear" the human.[13] But there is a sense in which God may "recognize" or show respect to the community of religious Jews, and that is by giving them a special responsibility or mission. This brings up the doctrine of the giving of the Torah.[14] The Jewish sources teach that God has given the community a special responsibility by giving them the Torah (the Teaching or Way), which includes an array of divine commandments. Moreover, the sources claim that the Torah is applicable to all Jews, throughout their generations. Once God has given the Torah, it turns out that keeping the Torah (following the Way) becomes a primary (if not *the* primary) act of reverence for God on the part of the Jewish people. The notion that God has given the Torah to the Jewish people is part and parcel of the Jewish conception of the good relationship with God. More on the notion of Torah later.

How does God express love for the Jewish community? God expresses love for the religious community through the providence of material and spiritual blessings, in this life and/or the next world. Material blessing includes physical health and well-being, flourishing and prosperity.[15] Spiritual blessing includes God's revelation and communication to the community. Thus, the giving of the Torah is an expression not only of God's recognition, but also of God's love.[16] Again, once God has given the Torah, keeping the Torah is a primary (if not *the* primary) act of love for God on the part of the Jewish people. Furthermore, spiritual blessing includes God's assisting the community to attain certain spiritual virtues or good qualities, such as holiness and righteousness. However, the greatest expression of God's love occurs when God is spiritually intimate with that community. Scripture refers to this as the "indwelling of the divine presence" amidst the Jewish people.[17] This is the divine response to the Jewish attempt to attain a bond (*devekut*) with God.

We may understand this relationship on analogy with an intimate relationship between two human beings. In a relationship of mutual recognition and love, two persons may bond with each other so closely, such that the values and aspirations, joys and sorrows, trials and tribulations, of the one person are in some way sympathetically experienced by the other person. Such a relationship is a partnership, in which the two partners share or participate in the personhood and/or personality of the other person. This partnership does not obliterate the distinction between the personhood of the two partners. Similarly, the religious community "bonds" with God, and

God "dwells within" that community, when God's projects and plans are shared and endorsed by the community, and when God's Supreme Personhood and/or Personality is expressed or exhibited through the community.

We must now return to clarify a point bypassed earlier. The doctrine that God has given the Torah logically implies or presupposes the doctrine of chosenness. For the Torah itself teaches the doctrine of chosenness. Hence, if it is true that God gave the Torah to the Jewish people, it then follows that God chose them for a special purpose. The significance of this point will emerge later. It is debatable whether the doctrine of chosenness somehow implies the divine origin of the Torah. It seems possible to characterize the doctrine of chosenness without necessarily mentioning the giving of the Torah. Theoretically at least, it seems God could have chosen the Jewish people for some special purpose, without giving them the Torah. However, this is an issue we need not here enter.

Two further points of clarification are necessary. The sources teach that while it is in some sense always true that God recognizes, loves, and dwells within the community of Jews, it is not always the case that this recognition, love, and "indwelling" is fully expressed or actualized. The notion of *galut* or "exile" is that God's presence is in some way missing from the Jewish people.[18] Thus, the material and spiritual blessings described above are conditional on how the Jewish people act over the course of history (primarily, it depends on whether they keep the Torah). Nevertheless, the sources emphasize that no matter how bad that relationship has become, the community has the opportunity to re-establish a good relationship with God.[19] The goal of the religious community is to attain a *fully expressed* or *fully actualized* relationship of mutual recognition, love, and bonding between God and the Jewish community.

Secondly, the Jewish teaching of chosenness does not entail that non-Jews have no capacity to establish a good relationship with God. On the contrary, Jewish sources teach that God recognizes all humans by giving them basic moral responsibilities, and by expecting that they fulfill them.[20] Furthermore, God manifests some form of love for all humans, indeed all creatures, by sustaining their existence, and allowing them to grow and flourish.[21] However, what is distinctive about the relationship between God and the Jewish people is that it involves the above described communal bond (*devekut*), which consists in an especially intense form of mutual respect/ recognition and love.[22] The Jewish sources indicate that the only way for non-Jews to be fully a part of this communal project is to join the Jewish people by making a commitment to follow the Torah. More on that point later.

So much for an account of the good relationship between God and the Jewish community. Within this context, what is the goal of the individual religious Jew? Basically, the individual seeks to recognize, fear, revere, love, worship and establish a bond with God, by keeping the Torah. But he or she does not pursue an exclusively private relationship between himself and God. Rather, the goal is to attain and maintain a relationship with God, *as a member of the religious community*. Similarly, God seeks to recognize, love, and "dwell within" each individual religious Jew, insofar as he or she is a member of the religious community. From the Jewish perspective, it is simply impossible for a solitary individual Jew, no matter how religious, to recognize, love and bond with God in the way that the religious community as a whole might do so. To the extent that the individual Jew participates in the divine-communal project of expressing the personhood or personality of God, it may be said that God "dwells within" that individual Jew.

Two further points must be added regarding the *kind* of value at stake in the relationship of *devekut* with God. We made similar points in Chapter 3 regarding the "generic" religious theist's conception of the good relationship with God, but they are worth repeating and refining in the context of Judaism.

First, the Jewish sources affirm that *devekut* with God is both *subjectively valuable* and *objectively valuable*. To say that *devekut* is subjectively valuable is to say that it involves or causes pleasure or joy.[23] To say that the relationship is objectively valuable involves two things, which we may call, *goodness* and *rightness*. Roughly, "goodness" is a feature of one's state or condition, and "rightness" is a feature of one's actions or behavior. The Jewish sources indicate that *devekut* with God is *good* insofar as it involves the well-being or flourishing of the persons who have attained that relationship.[24] But the sources also teach that the relationship with God is objectively valuable insofar as it involves doing (or having done) what is *right*, that is, fulfilling (or having fulfilled) one's *duty* or *obligation*.[25] The Jewish sources teach that *devekut* with God is valuable in all of these ways.

Secondly, inasmuch as God is conceived as supreme, so too the relationship of *devekut* with God is conceived by the Jewish sources as having supreme worth or value for the religious person who attains it. The argument given in Chapter 3 can be reiterated. In the relationship of bonding with God, the religious person (as a member of the religious community) shares or participates in God's Supreme Personality and/or Personhood.[26] Thus the relationship with God is conceived not merely as "a lot better" or "vastly better" than any other goal, but as qualitatively superior to any other goal. Differently stated, *devekut* with God is conceived as better in kind than any other conceivable good a human might have; no quantitative amount of other goods (that is, goods that a human might have independently of a good relationship with God) added together would equal the value of that relationship for that human. Furthermore, putting this point together with the previous one, *devekut* is conceived as supreme both subjectively and objectively, in the ways just described above. A person who attains *devekut* attains a state that involves or causes supreme joy or pleasure, *and* that involves or causes supreme well-being or flourishing, *and* in which he is doing or has done that which is supremely right to do. However, it is worth noting that the religious Jew need not have all this in mind whilst he is going about his pursuit of *devekut*. We shall return to this point later.

This concludes our sketch of the Jewish conception of the good relationship with God. It is the task of Jewish philosophical theology to work out the details of that relationship. Questions arise such as, what, if anything, is the *most important* aspect of our relationship with God? Is reverence more important than love, or *vice versa*? Or, are they both equally important? Is it the intellectual/cognitive aspects, that is, our knowledge of God that is most important? Is it the emotional aspect, the "feeling" of reverence and love? Is it perhaps the more pragmatic aspects of our relationship that are more important, that is, the way that we *act*, regardless of our state of mind or intent? What matters more, pursuing religious well-being, or just doing what is right because God commands it? How are the two related? What about service of God out of the desire for spiritual pleasure or joy? Is there something wrong with that? What is spiritual pleasure or joy in the first place? Another area of inquiry is what does God gain, if anything, out of this relationship with the Jewish people? Jewish theologians have discussed and debated such questions for centuries. It has not been our aim here to work out that notion in full detail, but only to articulate a conception of the good relationship with God, which differentiates Judaism from other religions.

We may now consider whether this conception of the good relationship with God is conceptually plausible. As stated earlier, it is rationally defensible for a person to have some conception if it is internally coherent and if it fits with related conceptions. In Chapter 3 we defended the rational coherency of the basic theistic conception of the good relationship with God as interpersonal and as supremely valuable. Is the Jewish *variation* on that concept also rationally defensible? The only thing we can do aside from articulating the notion itself is to consider some objections to that conception. Of course, it is impossible to consider all possible objections. In what follows I shall describe and respond to two common objections.

The first objection concerns the Jewish claim that the good relationship with God is inherently *communal*. As noted earlier, the sources teach that the good relationship can take place only between God and the community of religious persons. But, given that God is conceived as Supreme, both in power and benevolence, why can't God relate just as well with individual persons on an individual basis? Assuming there is some answer to this question, another standard objection concerns the Jewish teaching of chosenness. The Jewish sources claim that God is not only the God of the Jews but also the God of all creation and all peoples. Why then wouldn't the Supreme Person seek to establish the same good relationship with all peoples?

At this juncture, some Jewish philosophers might be inclined to appeal to "divine mystery." In response to such objections, one might be tempted to say that *we simply don't know* why the relationship is communal or what is the need for a chosen people. The fact that we don't know the answer to these questions does not render these doctrines incoherent. We may label this the "pietist" approach. However, the appeal to divine mystery is not valid as a response to apparent incoherencies in one's religious conceptions. The problem regarding chosenness, for example, is precisely that the notion of an all-powerful and all-good God who chose a special people for a special relationship seems *incoherent*. The appeal to divine mystery is inappropriate as a response to this objection. (Similarly, if one were to assert that God has some property and the negation of that property, the pietist could not legitimately escape this logical contradiction by asserting that it is a "divine mystery.")

At the same time, in order to respond successfully to such objections, all one needs is to show that these objections do not succeed in identifying some incoherency in the doctrine at issue. One does not need to come up with *the definitive answer* for why God has done what he is claimed to have done.[27] Rather, all one needs to come up with is some *speculation* for why God might have done what one claims he has done. This will be enough to defuse the objection. The following is an attempt to supply such a "speculation."

In response to the first objection above, the Jewish sources do not insist that all individual or solitary relationships between individuals and God are worthless. Rather, Judaism insists that specifically the relationship of bonding (*devekut*) with God requires a community of like-minded religious individuals. Earlier it was suggested that the community bonds with God when God's projects and plans are fully shared and endorsed by the community, and when God's Supreme Personhood or Personality is expressed or exhibited through the community. Much like any other grand human achievement, the attainment of that special relationship with God is not something that an individual can do on his own. For example, we said earlier that one of the ways in which this project is carried out is by living a moral life. But living a moral life is a social endeavor, not strictly an individual one. Furthermore, there are certain moral and spiritual virtues that are inherently social (for example, justice, righteousness, generosity). In general, "walking in God's way" is not something one can do all on one's own. It seems eminently plausible to conceive of this project as inherently communal.

The second objection above concerns the teaching of *chosenness*. In response, it is first necessary to keep in mind that the apparent harshness of this teaching is mitigated by another Jewish tenet, namely, that converts are accepted into the Jewish people.[28] The doctrine of chosenness is *not* that God exclusively chose one *race* for the purpose of establishing a certain relationship. Nevertheless, conversion to Judaism involves not just the adoption of a religion, but also joining the Jewish people. Thus it remains that the Jewish sources teach that God especially chose one special people or nation. Is it plausible that God might have done this?

To this question there are various possible responses. One response is that God chose to establish the good relationship with the Jewish people as an intermediate step toward eventually establishing that same relationship with all peoples. On this view, chosenness is a means to an end. Another response is that, based on our discussion of love and respect, the dynamics of love are such that (even) God can be intimate only with a particular community of persons rather than with the entire class of human persons.[29] That is, while God can respect and be respected by all persons, he can establish a relationship of intimate love only with a particular community of persons.

Another response is to try to deduce a rationale for the chosenness of a people from the rationale above for the communal nature of *devekut*. Perhaps the communal nature of *devekut* requires a relatively close-knit group of persons who are tied together by common history and peoplehood.

Another, related, response is that while God chose to relate to the Jewish people in a certain distinctive way, God also wishes to relate well with other peoples, albeit in different ways. The notion that God wishes to relate well with all humans is implicit in the teaching that God issued a universal code of behavior for all humans.[30] Perhaps it is part of the divine scheme that the world be populated by a variety of peoples with a diversity of dispositions and talents; each people has some divine purpose or mission which it is supposed to accomplish. Within this multi-cultural context, it is conceivable that God chose the Jewish people to play a pivotal role in establishing a good relationship between God and all peoples. That pivotal role involves attaining the intimate relationship of bonding (*devekut*) with God. To enable them to play that role, God has given the Jewish people the Torah, which includes, but also surpasses, the universal code that God expects all humans to follow.

In short, the doctrine of chosenness need not be viewed as a doctrine of *exclusion*, but rather as a doctrine of *mission*. In order to fulfill that mission, certain privileges, but also certain responsibilities are bestowed on the Jewish people. Any individual who wishes to adopt that mission is welcome to do so, provided one commits oneself to joining the chosen people.

In summary of this section, we have said that in order to be a religious Jew, a person must conceive of *devekut* as a supremely valuable goal. We have also attempted to defend this notion as conceptually plausible by responding to two common objections. Before moving on, we must raise the following question. What is the religious Jew committed to regarding other, competing notions of the good relationship with God, such as those espoused by other religions? No doubt, he will find *some* competing notions of that relationship to be incoherent. But, the religious Jew may conceivably admit that *some* competing conceptions of that supremely valuable relationship are coherent. In order for it to be rationally defensible for a person to have a Jewish conception, he need not think that this conception is the *only* coherent one. We shall return to this point later.

4.4 The Jewish Conception of the Religious Way: The Torah

The third condition for being a religious Jew is that one must have a Jewish conception of the *religious way*, that is, a Jewish conception of *how* to attain or maintain the good relationship with God. What is the Jewish conception of the way? Stated simply, the way to pursue that goal is to follow or "observe" the Torah. As stated earlier, the Torah is purported to be God's teaching, including his commandments upon the Jewish people, applicable to all Jews throughout their generations. Thus, the Jewish conception of the religious way is integrally linked with its conception of the religious goal. As stated above, the good relationship involves God's recognition and love of the Jewish community, which is expressed partially in that God has given them the Torah. But the sources also teach that the Torah itself is God's prescription for *how* the Jewish people, throughout their generations, should pursue that relationship. Hence, the Torah is central both to the Jewish conception of the relationship with God, as well as to the Jewish conception of the way to attain, maintain, and improve that relationship.

Let us elaborate briefly on the conception of the Torah or "teaching." Rabbinic literature teaches that God has communicated not only the Written Torah, which is contained in the Hebrew Scriptures, but also the Oral Torah, which is expressed in the rabbinic literature.[31] Included in the Written and Oral Torah is a system of divinely ordained law, that is, a set of societal norms which God has commanded upon the Jewish people, especially through Moses, but also through the interpretations and enactments of other prophets and sages. The written portion of the Law is contained in the Pentateuch; the Oral Law is expressed in the rabbinic literature. Both the Written and Oral Torah include historical accounts, homiletic materials, parables, ethical instructions, psalms, prayers, words of wisdom, and so on. Thus, a religious Jew conceives of "following the Torah" not only in the narrow sense of obeying Pentateuchal and rabbinic law, but also in the broad sense of living in accord with the values and ideals of the entire teaching.

The notion that God has given the Torah has raised many questions about the nature of divine revelation and its expression in sacred literature. Such questions include: does the notion that God gave the Torah to Moses mean that God dictated certain specific words which the prophet Moses heard and then wrote down? Or, can it mean that God inspired Moses in a certain way, such that Moses wrote down words that resulted from his own imagination? Do the Jewish sources teach that each and every word of the Pentateuch was dictated to Moses? Even if every word was originally dictated to Moses, is it also taught by the Talmud that the present text of the Pentateuch is exactly identical with Moses' text? Are all the claims and doctrines that are taught in the Pentateuch, the Scriptures, and the Talmud to be taken as literally true? Or, are some claims to be understood metaphorically? Furthermore, despite the notion that God intends the Torah to be applicable to the Jewish people throughout their generations, is there room for development, evolution, or adaptation of the law over time? These are only some of the questions raised by the notion of the Torah. We shall return to some of these questions later. Insofar as the classical Jewish sources are open to different responses, there may be a number of possible *variations* on the Jewish conception of the Torah. Minimally, on the present proposal, for a conception of the religious way to count as Jewish, it must involve the notion that the relationship of bonding (*devekut*) between the Jewish people and God is advanced by following the Torah.

In summary so far, we have articulated the Jewish conception of the religious way in a way that fits with the Jewish conceptions of God and the good relationship with God. Not surprisingly, even a brief study of the contents of the Torah indicates that it includes all those things that one would expect to find in a theistic religious way that rests on a claim of revelation. As part of the religious way, the Torah requires a) cognitive/spiritual activities such as meditation, contemplation, and prayer,[32] b) moral behavior,[33] c) study of God's revelation,[34] and, more generally, d) acting in accord with God's revealed directives about how to live rightly and about how to attain, maintain, and improve the good relationship with God.[35]

It remains to defend the conception of the Torah as the religious way against certain standard objections. Historically, the Jewish conception of Torah has been attacked in different ways. It is impossible here to mention and respond to all such challenges. In the remainder of this chapter, we shall consider three common objections to the coherency of the notion of the Torah as the religious way. In each case, we shall sketch some of the strategies that may be used to defuse these objections. However, a full discussion of these issues goes beyond our scope. Our aim here is only to show that these commonly raised objections do not show that conception of Torah as the religious way is *incoherent*.[36]

The first objection claims that there are apparent inconsistencies within the text of the Hebrew Scriptures. Certain passages seem to contradict others. For example, on the surface it seems that Genesis contains two versions of the account of creation. If indeed the text of the Torah is inconsistent, could it still be coherent to suppose that the Torah is divinely revealed or that it constitutes the religious way?

In response, recall that the Torah includes not only the Hebrew Scriptures, but also the Oral Torah, which includes rabbinic exegesis. One task of exegesis is to resolve apparent inconsistencies in the Scriptures. A general point about texts is relevant here. For any text that contains apparent inconsistencies, it is always possible that there is some resolution to be theorized. Moses Maimonides went so far as to claim that the prophets *knowingly* introduced inconsistencies into the Scriptural text for various pedagogical reasons.[37] Hence, the fact that there are apparent inconsistencies in the plain meaning of Scripture does not imply that God did not reveal the Torah. Nor does this render incoherent the notion that the way to attain a certain relationship with God is by following the Torah.

The second objection focuses on the Torah as a system of law. Is it coherent to think that God would have deemed it necessary to legislate a divine law, in order to establish a good relationship with the religious community? Why could God not have simply recommended, or perhaps commanded, those actions which promote the good relationship with God, without legislating a body of religious law?

In response, the Jewish sources insist that man is not only a social animal, but a legal animal as well. The religious character of the Jewish community is not sufficiently defined merely by its customs and rites. What binds the community together and propels it toward a certain relationship with God is the code of law by which that community lives. Indeed, any community is held together by some system of rules and regulations; the most fundamental of which is, arguably, its legal code. For it is ultimately the law that defines what behavior is acceptable or unacceptable in a given society, partly by defining what sanctions will be employed to enforce those rules and regulations. Hence the plausibility of a religious law.

A third objection is based on the assumption that all human beings have some natural capacity to know what is morally right or wrong. We know (somehow) that justice, compassion and benevolence are good; injustice, cruelty, and greed are bad. Why, then, is it not sufficient that religious persons establish a good relationship with God simply by living a morally good life? What sense can be made of the many rituals in the Torah, such as animal sacrifices? Is it coherent to think that such practices will lead to a good relationship with God? Furthermore, the Torah prescribes a number of things that seem not only peculiar, but also downright unjust. For example, certain punishments for certain transgressions seem unusually harsh. For instance, the punishment for committing adultery is death. Another troublesome issue, especially for many moderns, concerns the role of women in the Torah. For example, it seems the Torah provides women with fewer rights and privileges than men, at least in certain respects. Is it coherent to suppose that the Supreme Being would have prescribed a way of life which conflicts with our sense of justice?

In response, three strategies have been used to counter such objections. These are what might be called the *pietist*, the *apologetist*, and the *developmentalist* strategies. Here we can only sketch each of these strategies in brief. It is the task of Jewish philosophy to work out these strategies in greater detail, and perhaps even to work out some subtle combination of all these strategies. However, for the present purpose, if any one of these strategies works, the stated objection is defused.

The pietist strategy runs as follows. Perhaps it is true that human beings have some innate capacity to know that certain actions are morally right or wrong. But it is not necessarily true that humans instinctively know *everything* about how humans ought to live, especially concerning how to establish an interpersonal relationship with God. It is quite plausible that, for the sake of attaining this relationship, God might command certain actions that we would never know of *without* revelation. It is also plausible that there be some commandments, whose reasons we do not fully understand and never will. Arguably, the presumption that humans should be capable of thoroughly understanding God's commands is not only mistaken but hubristic as well.

Furthermore, the pietist strategy insists it is not surprising if the Torah prescribes some things that seem unjust. It is rationally defensible to suppose that our own sense of what is just is not perfect, and that God may very well know better than we what is just or unjust. Thus, suppose it does seem unjust to us that the punishment for adultery is death, or that God should have arranged matters such that women have fewer privileges than men. The pietist response is that it is still coherent to think that there could be some divine purpose at work here, which we fail to understand because of our limited abilities. The fact that we do not comprehend everything in the Torah does not imply that it is incoherent to think that the Torah is the way to a good relationship with God.

The pietist approach appeals to divine mystery. This approach is more appropriate here than earlier when we faced the problem of chosenness. It is one thing to assert there could be some things we don't understand about the *details* of God's commands, or even to assert that *some* of the commands conflict with our intuitive sense of fairness. However, perhaps the pietist response would fail if the *vast bulk* of the commandments conflicted with our intuitive sense of justice. Similarly, it seems the pietist response is insufficient to defuse the objection that God's selection of a special people conflicts with our sense of justice. For this calls into question the plausibility of the giving of the Torah to a chosen people, rather than the plausibility of some of its details.

In any case, not everyone will find the pietist strategy appealing. The apologetist strategy is to articulate some rationale to "explain away" those rituals and laws that seem peculiar or unjust. For example, one might argue that bringing animal sacrifices reinforces the notion that God expects a high level of devotion; or that it allows the religious Jew to experience an intimacy with God by partaking in a meal at which God is symbolically present. Similarly, one might theorize that God intended the relationship between husband and wife as a model for the relationship that God aims to establish with the Jewish people. From this perspective, it is not unreasonable to view adultery as a profound violation of the divine intention. It is also not unreasonable that the husband has certain privileges (and also certain responsibilities), which the wife lacks. Of course, this conception of the roles of husband and wife may conflict with certain modern ideas about those roles. But this would show only that the Torah is externally incoherent with certain conceptions of those roles which are foreign to the Torah.

Not everyone will find the apologetist strategy appealing. The developmentalist strategy runs as follows. Earlier we mentioned the question of to what extent the application of the Torah may evolve over time. In truth, within the Talmud itself certain portions of scriptural law are circumvented and in some cases done away with completely. Clearly, Jewish law does undergo development. For example, the Talmud teaches that the actual circumstances under which the death penalty could be carried out are extremely rare.[38] It is also the case that although Scripture permits a man to have more than one wife, the rabbis banned this practice during a later period.[39] How could the rabbis do this? According to the Talmud, God empowered the rabbis and sages of each age to interpret, and if necessary, adapt the Torah so that its basic principles are applied. The Talmud makes clear that if necessary, the rabbis have the power to "uproot" certain things from the Torah, and to impose certain injunctions to defend or secure the Torah.[40] They have the power to do this if they find that in some circumstances, certain aspects of the law come into conflict with certain other aspects of the law. When and whether this is appropriate is a question of judgment that must be decided by the community of Torah scholars. On such questions, there is of course room for debate among Torah scholars; there is also a mechanism in place for settling such debates.

Using this approach, one might argue that while certain punishments for certain transgressions may have been appropriate at some time in the past, they are no longer appropriate now. Similarly, some Jewish thinkers have claimed that while animal sacrifices may have been appropriate in the past, they are no longer appropriate and will never be appropriate. Similarly, one might argue that while a subservient role for women may have been appropriate in earlier times, it is no longer appropriate now. One might even try to make the case that women should be given the exact same privileges and rights as men; the latter is a matter of debate among current Jewish writers. It is not our business here to settle such debates. The point here is that there exists a mechanism in Torah law by which the rabbis can adapt its application to changing circumstances, if there are good reasons, based on the Torah itself, for doing so. A law that is deemed to conflict with some other law, or with principles of equity and justice, can be restricted, emended, or even uprooted. Since this mechanism is built in to the Torah, any such incoherence can, in theory, be resolved.

We have discussed several strategies of response to some common objections against the coherence of the conception of the Torah as the religious way. Granted, not everyone will find any or all of the above strategies satisfying. It will always be theoretically possible that the above objections could be refined and reformulated in a more convincing manner, and other objections could be raised as well. It is the task of Jewish philosophy to address such objections as they arise, and to work out strategies of response such as those described above. The claim here is that, to date, no compelling objection has ever been offered which shows that the Jewish conception of the religious way is incoherent.

Finally, what is the religious Jew committed to thinking about *other* conceptions of the religious way? With regard to his own particular conception of the religious end, namely, *devekut*, the religious Jew is committed to thinking that no other alternative religious way is plausible as a means toward that end. The conception of the end (*devekut*) is inextricably bound up with the conception of the means (Torah). However, the religious Jew might very well concede that some *other* kind of interpersonal relationship with God might conceivably be attained through some *other* religious way. We shall return to this issue later.

4.5 The Belief in the Live Possibility of God (On the Jewish Conception)

We now turn to the fourth condition for being a religious Jew, namely, the *belief that there is (at least) a live possibility that there is a God (on the Jewish conception)*. Above we claimed that the Jewish concept of God *just is* the basic concept of God articulated earlier. If this is correct, no new argument is required to support the rational defensibility of Condition 4. There is sufficient empirical evidence to justify the belief in the live possibility of God according to the Jewish conception.

Of course, if one *adds* to the basic God-concept certain features, then one would need more argument to support (even) a minimal belief in such a God. For example, if the Jewish theologian insists that for example, the property "God of Abraham" is an essential feature of his concept of God, then, fresh argument will be needed to support the (minimal) belief in God so conceived. Such argument might consist in evidence, or in a conceptual argument about why the property "God of Abraham" follows from other properties in the basic God-concept. However, here we have adopted the view that the Jewish concept *just is* the basic God-concept. Hence, no further argument is necessary to support the (minimal) belief that there is a God according to the Jewish conception.[41]

Some students of Judaism may be inclined to object that, from the perspective of the Jewish sources, the condition that one believes there is (at least) a live possibility that there is a God is either 1) *too strong* or 2) *too weak*. That is, one might think that, based on the sources of Judaism, to be a religious Jew one need not have *even* this minimal belief. There is a view prevalent in some quarters that Judaism does not have any "dogmas," and that somehow one can be a religious Jew without having *any* beliefs at all.[42] On the other extreme, some students of Judaism might object that it is not *sufficient* to count as a religious Jew unless one has a *confident* belief in certain tenets.[43] The position advocated in this book represents a middle position between these two extremes. It is necessary to respond to both objections.

First, let us respond to the objection that Condition 4 is *too strong*. The proposal at the start of this book was that a religious person is someone who pursues a certain relationship with God. We have already argued that engaging in this pursuit logically requires or presupposes a minimal belief that there is a God. In this part, we proposed that a religious Jew be defined as someone who pursues a certain specific relationship (*devekut*) with God in a certain specific way (through keeping the Torah). It follows as a matter of simple logic that the religious Jew is rationally committed to having *at least* a minimal belief in God. Of course, one could start out with a different proposal for how to define a religious Jew. One might try to define the religious Jew in such a way that it does not involve keeping the Torah, but what would be the motivation for doing so? On the other hand, one might try to define a religious Jew strictly as one who *acts* in a certain way, regardless of what one intends or hopes to achieve by those actions. But, again, that "way" would presumably involve keeping the Torah. And, ostensibly, keeping the Torah involves the pursuit of a relationship with God. Hence, the minimal belief condition described in Condition 4 is not too strong after all.

Next, let us consider the objection that Condition 4 is *too weak*. Surely, one could start out by defining a religious Jew as someone who has full confidence in a certain set of religious tenets or doctrines. But one would have to support this somehow. Many Jews who consider themselves religious and who act in an otherwise religious manner simply do not have a confident belief that there is a God or that the Torah is divinely given. There is no compelling reason to label these people as "non-religious Jews" if they keep the Torah and consider themselves to be pursuing a good relationship with God, even in the face of their doubts.

Someone who wishes to press this objection might insist that from the very start, we should define the religious Jew as *someone who keeps the Torah*, and then try to argue that the Torah mandates having certain beliefs. Moses Maimonides, for example, held that the Torah requires certain beliefs, and that one who does not have these beliefs is in some sense out of the fold.[44] Despite Maimonides' efforts, the claim that the Torah mandates certain beliefs is not entirely easy to discern based on the Scriptures and Talmud.[45] The Torah clearly mandates certain physical and verbal actions, and arguably certain attitudes or emotions (love and reverence of God). Additionally, the Talmud makes clear that it is forbidden to *deny* overtly certain doctrines.[46] Still, the question about whether it mandates beliefs *per se* is controversial.

But let us suppose for the sake of argument that the case can be made that the Torah mandates beliefs. Still, one might agree with the notion that the Torah *requires beliefs*, without agreeing that the Torah requires that they be held *with full confidence*. The view defended here is that one meets the minimum standard by having at least a minimal belief in certain basic dogmas. Furthermore, one may concede that the Torah requires certain beliefs, even confidently, yet hold that the criterion for what counts as a "religious Jew" does not, and indeed cannot, include obedience to the entire

Torah. After all, very few religious Jews fulfill the whole Torah; yet we would not say there are very few religious Jews. Perhaps it is reasonable to say that a person counts as a religious Jew so long as he keeps *a significant portion* of the Torah. If so, someone who lacks a confident belief in God but keeps a significant portion of the Torah (to the extent applicable to him) would still count as a religious Jew.[47]

Finally, it should be made clear that on the view endorsed in here, a Jew who believes *merely* in the live possibility of God's existence or reality lacks a component which is necessary for attaining a good relationship with God. In this respect, the position adopted here agrees to some extent with Maimonides' position. In fact, the conception of *devekut* is such that, in the end, the religious Jew is supposed not just to believe, but to *know* there is a God. So, the effort to attain knowledge of God is itself part of the goal of keeping the Torah. From this perspective, it is certainly *better* for the religious Jew to have a *confident* belief that there is a God rather than a minimal belief. However, the key point remains that in order to *pursue* that relationship, one need not *already* be in the position of knowing, or even confidently believing, that there is a God. This position disagrees with that of Maimonides to the extent that it does not write off a doubting Jew as a "heretic." So long as one has a belief in the live possibility that there is a God (and so long as one fulfills the other conditions described in this part) one qualifies as a religious Jew.

4.6 The Belief that Following the Torah Promotes the Likelihood of *Devekut*

The religious Jew is committed to the belief that it is (at least slightly) more likely that he will attain or maintain *devekut* if he follows the Jewish religious way than if he does not. For, if he does not believe this, he could not be properly said to pursue *devekut* by following the Torah. Under what circumstances is it rationally defensible to have this belief?

Before proceeding, we need to take one step back. It follows from what has been said earlier that the religious Jew is committed to the belief that there is at least a live possibility that *God has chosen the Jewish people* and *God has given the Torah to the Jewish people*. Because, if these doctrines are false, there is no chance that the Jewish religious goal can be attained. And, in general, if a person pursues a goal *G* such that *G* is attainable only if *P* is true, then that person is rationally committed to believe there is at least a live possibility that *P*. (This is especially true where it is *obvious* that *G* is attainable only if *P*; or where the person himself *concedes* that *G* is attainable only if *P*.) Hence, in order to show that it is rationally defensible to be a religious Jew, one needs to show that it is rationally defensible to believe there is (at least) a live possibility that these doctrines are true.

As stated earlier, the doctrine of chosenness follows from the doctrine of the divine giving of the Torah to Israel. Hence, if it can be shown that there is (at least) a live possibility that God has given the Torah, it follows that there is (at least) a live possibility that the doctrine of chosenness is true. Based on earlier discussion,[48] if it is rationally defensible for a person to believe that 1) there is (at least) some small evidence for the proposition that *God has given the Torah to the Jewish people*, and that 2) there is no conclusive disproof of this proposition, then, it is rationally defensible for that person to believe there is (at least) a *live possibility* that this proposition is true. It is not too difficult to show that, for many persons, this two-fold criterion is indeed met.

First, it is rationally defensible for many persons to believe there is at least *some* evidence for the proposition that God has given the Torah to the Jewish people. The evidence is the ongoing existence of the Jewish tradition itself. Jews have possessed and practiced the Torah for centuries. The claim that the Torah has a divine origin is rooted in a further claim of a collective religious experience of divine revelation at Mount Sinai.[49]

Of course, one could argue that this evidence is too minimal to establish the truth of the claim that the Torah has a divine origin, but that is not our concern here. The point is there is at least some small evidence for the proposition that the Torah has a divine origin. To see this point, imagine a world in which there was no Jewish tradition, or in which the Jewish tradition was a relic of the ancient past, such that no religious Jews were alive today. In such a world, there would be *less* evidence than there is in our world for the claim that God gave the Torah as a means for establishing a relationship with the Jewish people. It follows that there is at least *some* small evidence in the actual world for this claim. The question of *how much* or *how substantial* is that evidence is a very interesting and contentious one, but it is one that we need not pursue for the purpose of this book.

Second, despite the commonly raised objections against the claim that the Torah is divine, it is notoriously difficult to disprove it conclusively. For example, it is sometimes thought that this proposition has been disproved by modern science, which (it is claimed) is inconsistent with the account of creation and miracles in Scripture. It is also sometimes thought that this proposition is inconsistent with modern biblical criticism, which claims to find historical errors and anachronisms in the Pentateuch, apparently indicating that the Pentateuch is not a divinely revealed text, but rather a human document that evolved over many centuries. Finally, it is sometimes claimed that the rise of Christianity provides counter-evidence to the Jewish doctrine that the Torah remains applicable to Jews in later generations.

However, even if all these arguments had merit, none of them show *conclusively* that the Torah is not divine or is no longer applicable to Jews. Briefly, there are several ways in which one might respond to the above arguments. First, one might reconcile the claims of modern science with those of Scripture by suggesting that science itself has not *proven* that creation and miracles do not occur; rather, science *assumes* that creation and miracles do not occur.[50] Alternatively, one might suggest that the scriptural account of creation and miracles may be read metaphorically rather than literally.[51] If so, there need not be any inconsistency between science and Scripture.

With regard to modern biblical criticism, analogues of the three defensive strategies described above in connection with an earlier objection are available. The *pietist* strategy insists that God could have miraculously revealed things to Moses that were ahead of Moses' time, and that God may have his inscrutable reasons for making the Pentateuch look like a human document, by intentionally inserting apparent historical flaws and anachronisms. Alternatively, the *apologetist* strategy is to consider each bit of biblical criticism and try to show that each apparent historical inaccuracy or anachronism is only an apparent one; that the philological, archeological, and anthropological analysis upon which biblical criticism is based is flawed or question-begging; that a careful reading of the Pentateuch shows that it does represent an integral whole which bespeaks a single author, and so on. Whether this strategy works or not will depend on the details of such arguments. Third, the *developmentalist* strategy would affirm that God did reveal the Torah to Moses, but concede that human hands have edited the Pentateuch during the course of its transcription, especially in ancient times.[52] During this period of transcription, perhaps certain anachronisms and historical inaccuracies may have crept into the text. One might even admit that there were different versions of the same original text, and that the text which we have now evolved or developed over time. Nevertheless, in spite of any such flaws, the Pentateuch as we know it represents that text which the Jewish community, under the leadership of its scholars and sages, accepted as canonical or binding at some pivotal point in their past. Whether or not there is good evidence for this developmentalist view of the Pentateuch is an issue we cannot settle here. The relevant point is that even if it could be shown that there are flaws and anachronisms in the current text of the Pentateuch, that would not *conclusively refute* the claim based on religious experience that both the Written and Oral Torah have a divine origin.

Finally, despite the advent and popular success of Christianity, it has never been conclusively proven that the Torah is no longer applicable to succeeding generations of Jews. Granted, there have been many Christians who claim to have experience of a God that has in some sense annulled the obligation of the Jewish people to keep the Torah. (Of course, there are many devout Christians who do not make this claim.) We need not pass judgment here on whether this constitutes *good evidence* against the claim that the Torah represents God's prescriptions for Jews of all generations. The relevant point is that it does not constitute *conclusive disproof*. Hence, the second criterion above is also met. In sum, it is rationally defensible to believe there is (at least) a live possibility that God has given the Torah to the Jewish people, and that it applies to Jews throughout their generations.

Let us return to the question at the start of this section. Is it rationally defensible for a person to believe that it is (at least slightly) more likely that he will attain or maintain *devekut* if he follows the Torah than if he does not? The strategy outlined earlier[53] may be applied here. We have already claimed that on the Jewish conception of *devekut*, it is only by following the Torah that one can attain *devekut*. This is because the religious end (*devekut*) is conceptually linked with the religious way (the Torah). We have also seen that there is (at least) some (small) evidence that *God gave the Torah* and no compelling evidence against it. It follows that it is rationally defensible to believe that it is more likely that one will attain *devekut* if one follows the Torah than if one does not. In addition, many Jews have claimed to have religious experience of attaining or partially attaining *devekut* with God, through keeping the Torah. This confirms the belief that following the Torah increases the probability (at least slightly) that one will attain *devekut*.

Before moving on, we must ask again, what view is the religious Jew committed to regarding the viability of alternative religious ways? Given what we have said, the religious Jew might very well allow that there is some probability that some *other* religious way may succeed in promoting a *different* "good relationship" with God other than *devekut*. For example, this would be the case if he thinks that there is some probability that the tenets of Christianity are true. We shall return to this issue later.

4.7 Following or "Keeping" the Torah

Finally, in order to qualify as a religious Jew one must engage in the way of life that is prescribed by the Torah. Before turning to the question of whether it is rationally defensible to do so, some preliminaries are in order.

First, it is obvious that some Jews are *more religious* or *less religious* than others.[54] Generally, a religious Jew keeps the Torah, or at least tries to, wherever and whenever applicable. A *very* religious Jew almost never fails an opportunity to keep the Torah, or at least, he tries at every turn. On the other hand, some religious Jews keep the Torah only on certain occasions. Is there a threshold of observance that a person must meet to count as a religious Jew? For the present purpose, we need not answer this question. It suffices to say that the degree of one's religiosity as a Jew varies to the extent that he or she keeps the Torah.

Furthermore, some religious Jews are *more devout* than others. This means that their motivation for acting religiously is more purely for its own sake, that is, for the sake of attaining or maintaining *devekut* with God. Those who pursue the goal of *devekut* only for the sake of some other motive are not devout.[55] Of course, many people have mixed motives for being religious Jews. Some may be religious partly out of habit or to avoid social censure or to maintain a family tradition. But they may also be religious partly out of the motive to attain a good relationship with God. Perhaps there are very few *purely devout* religious Jews. This is another issue that we need not here pursue.

Conceivably, a very religious Jew might not be very devout. Someone might keep the Torah as fully as possible, and pursue a relationship of *devekut* with God, for the sake of some ulterior motive such as one suggested above. However, quite arguably, it is one of the commandments to *serve God devoutly*.[56] If so, this person would *ipso facto* be deficient in his observance of at least one particular commandment. Hence his religiosity would be deficient after all. On the other extreme, we may wonder whether it is possible for someone to fulfill only a small number of commandments, yet do so very devoutly. It is questionable whether such a thing is psychologically possible or feasible given that the Torah constitutes a system of closely related and integrated commandments. Perhaps it could be argued that a *very devout Jew* would have to be *a very religious Jew*. But, again, this is another issue we need not settle here.

Against the present proposal, the following objection might be raised. Imagine a Jew who seeks to fulfill all or nearly all of the commandments of the Torah, *strictly out of a desire to obey God's commands*. Imagine that such a person, if asked, would *deny* that he fulfills the commandments in order to attain a good relationship with God. Suppose he insists that the only reason he fulfills the Torah is to obey God's commands. On the present proposal, the result follows that such a person fails to qualify as a religious Jew.[57] Is this an absurd result?

This objection poses the hypothetical possibility of a very religious Jew who consciously denies that he pursues the goal of *devekut*. If it is correct to say that the pursuit of *devekut* is one of the commandments,[58] then, the hypothesis itself is somewhat absurd. A Jew who seeks to fulfill *all* of the commandments would *ipso facto* pursue a good relationship with God. Moreover, if a Jew were to *deny* that he pursues a good relationship with God, he would be denying what the Torah teaches regarding the purpose of keeping the commandments. Based on the sources of Judaism, it would not be absurd to regard such a person as something other than a religious Jew.

It is worth recalling that, as mentioned earlier, to pursue *devekut* one need not pay much conscious attention to a) the spiritual joy or pleasure that might be had from attaining *devekut*, nor to b) the well-being or flourishing of the spirit that attends *devekut*. Analogously, a soccer player pursues the goal of getting the ball in the net, and enjoys doing so; but that does not mean he consciously pursues the *pleasure* or *joy* of getting the ball in the net. To pursue some goal for its own sake does not mean that one consciously pursues the *pleasure* or even the *goodness* that attends that goal. But the point remains that, on the present proposal, a person does not count as a religious Jew unless he pursues *devekut*.[59]

So much for preliminaries. Is it rationally defensible for someone to fulfill Condition 6? Let us restate the question as follows. Is it more rationally defensible for a person to follow or keep the Torah, *rather than to live a non-religious way of life?* We may apply the pragmatic strategy articulated in a general way in the previous part. We have already argued that it is rationally defensible for some persons to fulfill all the conditions heretofore described for being a religious Jew. Given such a person's conception of *devekut* with God as supremely valuable, and given his belief that the probability that he will attain it is increased only if he keeps the Torah, it follows that there is a higher expected value for him to keep the Torah rather than to live a non-religious life. In general, whenever and wherever there is a choice between keeping the Torah as opposed to not doing so, the option of keeping the Torah will have the higher expected value. It follows that it is rationally defensible for such a person to be a *very* religious Jew, rather than to be non-religious.

In summary of Chapter 4, a person is a religious Jew if and only if:

1 He has a Jewish conception of God, that is, as Supreme Person.
2 He conceives of the good relationship with God as *devekut*, that is, a relationship of mutual recognition and love between God and the Jewish people.
3 He conceives of the Torah as the way to attain or maintain that relationship.
4 He believes there is (at least) a *live possibility* that there is a God (according to the Jewish conception).
5 He believes that following the Torah promotes (*at least slightly*) the probability that he will attain or maintain *devekut*.
6 He follows or keeps the Torah.

We have also shown that it is rationally defensible for some persons to fulfill each and all of these conditions. Now, it seems possible that a similar argument might be constructed to provide a rational defense for some religion other than Judaism. What ramifications would such a competing argument have for the present argument in support of Judaism? Another way of raising the same issue is as follows. We have claimed that it is rationally defensible for a person (who fulfills Conditions 1–5) to be a religious Jew *rather than to be non-religious*. But this still leaves open the question whether it is more rationally defensible for such a person to keep the Torah, *rather than to pursue some other religious way*. This issue is addressed in the next, final, section.

4.8 Reflections on Religious Pluralism

This book has argued that it is rationally defensible for some persons to be religious theists, and, more specifically, that it is rationally defensible for some persons to be religious Jews. However, this book has not argued that it is rationally compelling upon all persons to be religious theists, much less, religious Jews. Moreover, nothing said in this book rules out the possibility that a persuasive argument might be constructed to show that some *other* religion aside from Judaism is rationally defensible for *other* persons. A similar argument might be constructed in defense of other versions of religious theism, such as Christianity, Islam, or certain versions of Hinduism, or even for non-theistic religions such as Taoism or Buddhism.

For example, the basic outline of the Christian version of the argument might run as follows. One would begin by articulating the Christian conceptions of God, the good relationship with God, and the religious way. One would explain why it is plausible to conceive of that relationship as supremely valuable. Then, one would argue there is sufficient epistemic reason or evidence to believe there is (at least) a live possibility both that the Christian God exists, and that, compared with a non-religious way of life, the Christian way is more likely to attain that relationship. One would also argue that there is sufficient epistemic reason to believe in the live possibility of those doctrines that must be true in order for a person to attain that relationship by living the Christian way. Finally, one would make the case that it is pragmatically rational to follow the Christian way, on the grounds that the potential value of that relationship is higher than that of any alternative option available to that person.

Something similar might be attempted even for non-theistic religions. Take Buddhism, for example. Instead of articulating a concept of God, one would articulate the goal of being a Buddhist (that is, the attainment of *nirvana* or enlightenment). One would explain why it is coherent to conceive of that goal as especially valuable or worthwhile to be attained. Next, one would articulate those propositions or doctrines that underlie Buddhism, that is, those doctrines which are required to be true in order for a person to reach the Buddhist goal. These would include certain doctrines regarding causation and the nature of suffering.[60] Next, one would try to show that a) there is (at least) some (small) evidence that those doctrines are true, and, b) living a certain Buddhist way of life (whatever that involves) increases the likelihood that one will attain the Buddhist goal. If the goal is conceived as supremely valuable, it will be rationally defensible to be a Buddhist even in the face of doubt about those doctrines.

In principle, there seems to be no reason why one could not construct a Christian (or Buddhist, or some other) version of the argument of Chapter 3 of this book. If so, one might then pose the question, is it more rationally defensible for a person to be a religious Jew, *rather* than a Christian (or Buddhist, or something else)? This takes us back to the problem of "other religions."[61] Now, in some instances, it might be rationally defensible for a person to *dismiss* a competing religion, if he has reason to think its conceptions of God, the good relationship with God, or the religious way are incoherent. In some instances, a person may come to the conclusion that the conception of the religious goal as supremely valuable makes more sense under one religion than it does under a competing religion. Alternatively, a person may be able to settle the issue if he judges that the evidence for the required doctrines underlying one religion is stronger than the evidence for the doctrines required by the other religion. Needless to say, different people will come to different conclusions on these matters.

However, suppose that a religious Jew *admits* that the conceptions involved in some alternative religion are logically coherent, and that the evidence for its doctrines is *just as strong* as the evidence for Jewish doctrines. In this case, would it *still* be more rationally defensible to choose Judaism over the competing religion?

In general, so long as a person conceives of *devekut* with God as supremely valuable, and believes that keeping the Torah increases the probability that he will attain *devekut*, it follows that he should keep the Torah rather than follow any other religious way. This inference holds even for a person who concedes that other religious paths are viable routes toward relationships with God *other* than *devekut*. Moreover, suppose a person concedes that it is logically coherent to think of some state other than *devekut* as supremely valuable. Nevertheless, so long as *he* conceives of *devekut* as the supremely valuable end, it will still be the case that it is rationally defensible *for him* to keep the Torah rather than pursue the alternative religious way. A similar point would hold (in reverse) for a Christian as well. Some explanation of this point is required.

As stated earlier, it is one thing to admit that some conception is *coherent*, and it is quite another to *have* a certain conception.[62] To *have* a certain conception of God or the good relationship with God is (among other things) to subscribe to the notion that a certain being or reality is *supreme*, and to the notion that a certain relationship with that being or reality would be *supremely valuable*. So, even though one might admit that a certain alternative conception of the good relationship with God is coherent, that does not mean one actually *has* that conception. For example, a religious Jew might admit that the Christian notion of having a good relationship with God through Jesus is coherent, but that does not mean that he *subscribes* to this conception. Similarly, a religious Jew might find the Buddhist notion of *nirvana* coherent, but that does not mean that he subscribes to it. For such a person, neither Christianity nor Buddhism constitutes a viable "competitor" to Judaism. Again, a similar point holds (in reverse) for the Christian or the Buddhist. The fact that a person concedes that some *other* conception of the supremely valuable end is coherent does not change the fact that *his* conception is *his*.[63]

Another relevant point is the following. Suppose a religious Jew grants that there is some small evidence for the doctrines of some alternative religion. Suppose for example that he grants there is some small evidence that the Torah has been revoked or superceded and that God initiated a "New Covenant," which is enshrined in the Christian Gospels. Still, it would not follow that he is rationally *compelled* to have even a minimal belief in such propositions. Earlier we argued that it is *rationally defensible* to have a minimal belief that *p* if one has some small evidence for *p* and no compelling evidence against it.[64] But we did not argue that it is *rationally compelling* for a person to have (even) a minimal belief that *p* under such circumstances. So, quite arguably, even if a religious Jew grants there is some small evidence for Christian doctrines, he is not rationally compelled to have (even) a minimal belief in their truth. And, if he lacks this minimal belief, Christianity is simply not a viable option for him. For, in such a case, he fails to fulfill one of the conditions for being a Christian, namely, having a minimal belief in those Christian doctrines that must be true in order for the Christian way to succeed. Again, a similar point may hold (in reverse) for a Christian. The fact that one concedes there is some evidence for some competing set of religious doctrines does not *rationally compel* one to have even a minimal belief in those doctrines. And, if one lacks those minimal beliefs, the competing religion does not constitute a viable option.

Having said all this, let us now consider a person who is confused or "torn" over his own conception of God and the good relationship with God. Suppose a person finds that he *subscribes* to the Christian notion of the good relationship with God, just as much as he *subscribes* to the Jewish conception of that relationship. Such a person finds two contrasting conceptions not only equally *plausible*, but also equally *appealing*. Suppose further that this person is confused or "torn" over his own belief in God. In other words, suppose he has a minimal belief not only that there is a God and that God has given the Torah, but also a minimal belief in the truth of those Christian doctrines which are necessary for the Christian religious goal to be obtained. Finally, suppose this person has engaged in study and reflection on both religions, and can find no conceptual or epistemic advantage in either one. For such a person, *both* Christianity and Judaism represent viable, yet competing, religious options. In such a case, the rational defensibility of choosing one religion *as opposed to the other* seems to dissolve. For such a person, *both* religions are equally rationally defensible!

As indicated earlier,[65] the situation just described is relatively rare. Competing religious traditions offer contrasting conceptions of the religious goal. Hence, most people will not be in the position of finding two competing religions to be *equally* plausible and appealing in the ways just described. But, assuming this situation were to occur, it would *still* be rationally defensible for such a person to follow *one* of these religious ways *rather than no religious way at all*. For, under such circumstances, a person would *still* have a rationally defensible belief that *either* of these two competing ways is more likely than any non-religious way to succeed at attaining a supremely valuable goal. Under such circumstances, it would be rationally defensible for a person to choose one of those two religious ways on the basis of other considerations (family ties, convenience, and so on) or even choose at random between those options. The point still holds that even under such circumstances, it is more rational to choose *one* of those religious ways *rather than some non-religious way altogether*.[66]

In sum, it would not be surprising if different religious philosophers, each working from within different religious traditions, were able to apply the strategy discussed in Chapter 3 in the effort to articulate a rational defense for adopting a different religion in each case. As we have seen, the conceptions that a person happens to have play a crucial role in which religion is most rationally defensible for that person. Not everyone has the same conceptions of God, the good relationship with God, and the way of attaining that relationship. It is clear that culture and tradition play a crucial role in determining or at least shaping one's conceptions. Furthermore, different people have different religious experiences that tend to support different religious beliefs (whether those beliefs are minimal or confident). It is perhaps a sociological truism that, as a general rule, a person brought up within a certain religious tradition tends to have beliefs and value commitments that are in sympathy with that tradition. By the same token, the mere fact that there are coherent religious alternatives is not in and of itself a reason for giving up one's own religion. This lends support to a certain form of *religious pluralism*, understood here as the thesis that *different religions, which make (some) conflicting claims, and involve (some) conflicting practices, can be rationally defensible for different persons.*

In this sense, religious pluralism does *not* entail that it is rationally defensible for *any* person to maintain allegiance to *whatever* religion in which he or she happens to have been inculcated. It is quite possible that some persons are engaged in religious ways that are *not* rationally defensible *for them*. For example, there might be some incoherence in their conception of God or the good relationship with God. Alternatively, it is possible that given some person's conception of the good relationship with God, the particular *way* which that person employs to pursue that relationship could turn out to be, on reflection, not the most plausible way of getting to that particular goal. Alternatively, it could be that the evidence typically cited in favor of some religious doctrine is fatally flawed. Such persons would be in a *more* rationally defensible position if they switched or at least modified either their religious conceptions and/or their religious way. Nevertheless, the fact that some persons are engaged in religions that are indefensible *for them* does not entail that *all* religions are indefensible *for everyone*.

Finally, in the sense used here, religious pluralism is not the absurd view that *all* religions are equally rational or valid *for everyone*. Rather, religious pluralism recognizes that, until and unless it can be shown that some particular religion is rationally compelling upon all rational beings, different religions may be rationally defensible for different persons. The same pluralistic point may hold for sects or groups within a given religion. Different sects or groups may have different variations on the same basic conceptions of God, the good relationship with God, and the religious way. This does not mean that theologians and philosophers should stop debating the coherency and probity of religious notions and doctrines. However, it does mean that such debates should be carried out in a spirit of tolerance.

Notes

1   This part is an expansion of my article "The Rational Defensibility of Being a Traditional Religious Jew" in *Religious Studies*, vol. 35 (December 1999) pp. 391–423.

2   Judaism is inherently a social religion, not an individual religion. Ideally, we should proceed not by defining what it is for some *individual* to be a *religious Jew*, but rather by defining what it means for a *group* of persons to be a *religious Jewish community*. Having done so, we could then ask whether it is rationally defensible for a group of persons to constitute themselves as a religious Jewish community. This would be a question about *collective* or *group* rationality. Having addressed that issue, we could then ask whether it is rational for some *individual* to join such a community. However, to avoid complexities about collective rationality, this book focuses more directly on the individual rather than the group. For better or worse, in doing so we are taking the standard approach in philosophy of religion of treating the question of whether it is rational to be a religious Jew as a question about *individual* rather than *group* rationality. Despite this, we shall find that the social nature of Judaism will inevitably emerge at various points in the discussion.

3   See Chapter 3, note 4.

4   Later we shall see that how one answers this question turns out to be immaterial to the argument of this book. See note 41 below.

5   *Mishna Sanhedrin*, 10:1.

6   See Jewish scriptural sources cited in Chapter 3, note 64.

7   In adopting this conception, we are not ruling out the notion the religious Jew may attain some great good caused by God, nor are we ruling out the notion of a next world or life after death. See below, note 23.

8   See non-Jewish sources cited in Chapter 3, note 64.

9   See Deuteronomy 10:1, 14:2.

10   On the communal nature of God's relationship with Israel, see Exodus 19:6, 25:8, and 29:46.

11   For a discussion of different types of fear/reverence for God, and different types of love of God, see the anonymous commentary [*perush*] on Moses Maimonides, *Code of Jewish Law*, Fundamentals of the Torah, II:I. See also, Moshe Hayyim Luzzatto, *Path of the Just* (Northvale, New Jersey: Jason Aronson, 1996) Chapter 24 and Schneur Zalman of Liadi, *Tanya*, Chs. 41–44.

12   See Deuteronomy 10:20: "You shall fear the Lord, your God; Him shall you serve, and you shall cleave [*tidbak*] to him." In later literature, the term *devekut* is sometimes used to connote a form of mystical union with God. However, this connotation is not necessarily implied in the Scriptural passage, and is not necessarily implied by our use of that term here. On this point, see Gershom Scholem's discussion of this term in *Major Trends in Jewish Mysticism* (New York: Schocken Books, 1974) p. 123. Scholem claims that for nearly all Jewish mystics, the height of spiritual attainment does not involve radical union. For a different view see Moshe Idel, *Kabbalah: New Perspectives* (New Haven: Yale University Press, 1988), Chapter 4.

13   The notion that God has fear or reverence (*yirah*) for the human is not found in the Hebrew Scriptures or in the rabbinic literature. However, we do find that under certain circumstances God expresses respect or honor (*kavod*) for the human being. See Samuel I, 2:30 and *Mishna Avot*, 4:1.

14   See Exodus 19–20.

15   See Leviticus 26:3–13; Deuteronomy 7:12–16; 28:1–14.

16   This notion is expressed in the daily Jewish liturgy in the blessings recited before the reading of the *Shema*. See *The Artscroll Siddur* (Brooklyn: Mesorah Publications, 1990) p. 88 and p. 258.

17   See Exodus 29:45.

18 See Deuteronomy 31:16 ff.

19 Deuteronomy 30; Maimonides, *Code of Jewish Law*, Laws of Repentance, 7:5.

20 *Sanhedrin* 56ff; Maimonides, *Code of Jewish Law*, Laws of Kings, 9.

21 The notion that God is the source of all beneficence (*hesed*) and goodness (*tov*) to all creatures is implicit in the creation story and in many other passages such as Psalms 104 and 145. The notion that God loves righteousness and justice is found in Psalms 33:5; that God loves the righteous, in Psalms 146:8.

22 Arguably, the Jewish sources teach that even the relationship between God and the Jewish people cannot be finally consummated or perfected except in the context of God's relationship with humanity at large. See, for example, Zechariah 14.

23 As cited in note 15, many scriptural verses support the notion of a material benefit (wealth, health, prosperity) for serving God. However, this seems to be a benefit that is conditional on communal observance. Cf. Maimonides, *Code of Jewish Law*, Laws of Repentance, 9:1. As far as the individual goes, it is not clear that there is any promise of a material benefit for *devekut*. Some sources indicate there is a spiritual pleasure or joy that the individual may experience by attaining a good relationship with God *in this world*. See for example, Isaiah 58:14. However, some rabbinical sources indicate that the full reward is *not* attained in this world. The Talmud states, "*Hayom la-asotam, u-machar lekabel secharam*" [= today is for doing them; tomorrow (that is, the next world) is for receiving their reward] (*Tractate Avodah Zarah* 4b). Cf., "*Sechar mitzvah, be-hai alma leka*" [= there is no reward for a commandment in this world] *Tractate Kiddushin*, 39b. One obvious resolution is the notion that *some portion* of the reward may be experienced in this world, but the full attainment is only in the next world.

24 Scriptural sources indicate that the relationship with God is good (*tov*) for Israel. See, for example, Psalms 34:9. This too might only be fully realized in the next world. See Maimonides, *Code of Jewish Law*, Laws of Repentance, 8:1, 3. Incidentally, the scriptural and rabbinic passages mentioned in the previous note may be taken to refer not to pleasure but to this type of 'good' or *tov*. In some Jewish sources, one also finds the notion that one who pursues *devekut* pursues what is objectively good not only for oneself or for the Jewish community, but also what is good for the world and even for God himself. See the discussion of the concept of *tikkun* in Scholem, *Major Trends in Jewish Mysticism*, pp. 274–8.

25 Deuteronomy 10:20 states the imperative to serve God with reverence, to worship God, and to pursue *devekut* with God. Indeed, the case can be made that insofar as it is a commandment, the pursuit of *devekut* can be fulfilled *only* in this world, on the grounds that there is no free will in the next world.

26 The notion of sharing in God's supreme nature is discussed by Moshe Hayyim Luzzatto, *The Way of God*, I: 2: 1, 3.

27 A similar strategy is sufficient to address the "logical" version of the problem of evil. See above, Section 3.5 and Chapter 3, note 77. As long as one can come up with some *speculation* for why an omnipotent and omnibenevolent being or reality might allow evil, one has escaped the logical problem of evil even if one's speculation happens in fact to be false.

28 In a sense, Abraham may be regarded as the first convert to Judaism. See R. Judah's opinion in *Jerusalem Talmud: Bikurim*, 1:4.

29 For further discussion of this approach, see Joshua L. Golding, "Jewish Identity and the Teaching of Chosenness" in *Jewish Identity and the Postmodern Age*, Charles Selengut, ed. (St. Paul, MN: Paragon House, 1999), pp. 91–108.

30 See above, note 20.

31 For a discussion of Oral and Written law, see Moses Maimonides, *Code of Jewish Law*, Introduction and also the Introduction to his *Commentary on the Mishna*.

32 See Moses Maimonides, *Code of Jewish Law*, Laws of Prayer.

33 See Moses Maimonides, *Code of Jewish Law*, Laws of Character Traits (*Deot*).

34   See Moses Maimonides, *Code of Jewish Law*, Laws of Torah Study.
35   See Moshe Hayyim Luzzatto, *Path of the Just*, Chapter 1.
36   The objection that the claim that the Torah has a divine origin is conceptually *incoherent* is to be distinguished from the objection that this claim is empirically *false*. The latter sort of objection will be addressed later (Section 4.6).
37   Moses Maimonides, *Guide to the Perplexed*, Introduction.
38   See *Tractate Makkot*, 7a. For a discussion of the rather rigorous conditions under which the death penalty would be applicable, see Moses Maimonides, *Code of Jewish Law*, Laws of the High Court, 12:1–2. However, it should be noted that Orthodox Jews regard the Talmudic amelioration of the death penalty as an interpretation of scriptural intent, and not as a development or evolution of divine law.
39   See *Shulchan Aruch: Even Ha-ezer* 1:9–11. (The *Shulchan Aruch* or "Set Table" is one of the most widely accepted compendia of Jewish law.)
40   For example, the Talmud suggests a way to circumvent the scriptural law that all monetary debts held by private citizens are cancelled during the Sabbatical year; see *Tractate Gittin* 34a.
41   We shall see shortly that the religious Jew is committed to certain other beliefs about what God does or has done, and so, fresh evidence or argumentation will be required to support these minimal beliefs. The result is that, as far as the argument in this book goes, it is immaterial whether or not one thinks of these additional features as "definitional" of God, or rather as features that describe things that God does or has done. Either way, one will need some support for the (minimal) belief that God has these features or has done these things.
42   On the centrality of belief in traditional Judaism, see J. David Bleich's Introduction to *With Perfect Faith: The Foundations of Jewish Belief* (New York: Ktav, 1983). For a sustained argument that Judaism does *not* require belief in any precisely formulated creed, see Menachem Kellner, *Must a Jew Believe Anything?* (London: Littman Library of Jewish Civilization, 1999). The position adopted here falls somewhere between the views of Bleich and Kellner.
43   Apparently, this is Maimonides' position. See his *Commentary on the Mishna: Sanhedrin*, 10:1.
44   See ibid.
45   See Kellner's critical discussion of Maimonides' position in *Must a Jew Believe Anything?*
46   *Mishna Sanhedrin*, 10:1.
47   On the status of doubt in Judaism, see references above in Chapter 1, note 25.
48   See Section 3.5.
49   According to some rabbinic accounts, only certain parts of the Torah (such as the ten commandments, or possibly only the first two) were revealed directly by God to the people of Israel. The rest of the Torah was given to Moses, who transmitted it to the people. See *Tractate Makkot*, 23b–24a.
50   There is a vast literature on the relationship between science and religion. For one bibliography, see *Philosophy of Religion: Selected Readings*, M. Peterson et. al. eds (Oxford: Oxford University Press, 2001), p. 531.
51   However, see Joshua L. Golding, "On the limits of non-literal interpretation of Scripture" in *Torah U-madda Journal* (November 2001) edited by David Shatz.
52   For an exposition of this view, see David Weiss Halivni, *Revelation Restored* (Boulder, Co: Westview Press, 1997). Weiss Halivni claims to find ample support for this view within Scripture and rabbinic literature itself.
53   See the earlier discussion in Section 3.7.
54   See the earlier discussion in Section 2.4.
55   Those who keep the Torah *only* for the sake of some goal *other* than attaining a good relationship with God (for example, for the sake of keeping up appearances) do not even

count as "religious" on the present definition of the religious Jew. Their religiosity is a sham, since they do not pursue a good relationship with God at all. (However, see the point about deference to authority below, note 59.) This is to be distinguished from those who keep the Torah in order to attain a good relationship with God, yet for the sake of some ulterior motive. The latter are religious Jews, but not devout. If they keep the Torah *both* for the sake of attaining *devekut and* for the sake of some other motive, they are *partly* devout.

56   See, for example, Maimonides' discussion of the duty to worship God with love in *Code of Jewish Law*, Laws of Repentance, 10:1–3.

57   We considered a variation of this objection earlier in Section 2.2.

58   See sources cited above, notes 11, 12, and 56.

59   It is important to bear in mind that, as suggested earlier, an ordinary religious person might defer to a religious authority on what is the goal of his religious actions. Thus, in order to qualify as a religious Jew, a person need not be able to articulate what is the goal of keeping the Torah. (This is different from the case of the person who explicitly *denies* that the goal of keeping the Torah is *devekut*.) On the view adopted here, a person counts as a "religious Jew" if the authority to whom he defers says that the goal is *devekut*.

60   For discussions of Buddhist doctrines see Edward Conze, *Buddhism: Its Essence and Development* (New York: Harper, 1959) and David J. Kalupahana, *Buddhist Philosophy: A Historical Analysis* (Honolulu: University Press of Hawaii, 1976). It is arguable that some versions of Buddhism (such as Zen Buddhism) do not have any doctrines. For any religion that disdains the formulation of doctrines, it will be difficult, if not impossible, to formulate a rational defense using the strategy outlined in this book. By the same token, religions that disdain the formulation of doctrines tend to disdain the project of formulating a rational defense of religious commitment.

61   See the earlier discussion in Section 3.7, p. 83ff.

62   See the discussion of the difference between *thinking that some conception is coherent* vs. *having a certain conception* in Section 3.7, p. 84. See also the discussion of the difference between *thinking of some idea* and *having a certain conception* in Section 2.2, p. 18.

63   See the analogy involving the conception of marriage toward the end of Section 3.7.

64   See above, Section 3.5, p. 71.

65   See above, Section 3.7, pp. 83–84.

66   Alternatively, under such circumstances, perhaps the most rationally defensible choice for such a person would be to develop a religious way of life that incorporates elements of both religions, or, one that blends together those elements that both religions have in common. Still another option might be to analyze both religions critically until one could make a judgment about which tradition seems more conceptually plausible and/or probable.

Appendix: Comparison of the Standard and Alternative Conceptions of God's Ontological Category

This appendix considers some of the merits of the standard vs. the alternative conceptions of God's ontological category described above (Section 3.2). Recall that the standard conception takes God's essence as *a being*, and the divine attributes as properties of that being. On the other hand, the alternative conception takes God's essence as *Being*, and the divine attributes as principles or laws in accord with which the universe operates. Using criteria described earlier,[1] it will be argued here that the alternative conception is more plausible than the standard one. However, the argument of this book does not hinge on whether one prefers the alternative or the standard conception of God. Hence this discussion has been relegated to an appendix.

First, it is worth noting that many advocates of the standard conception of theism would *agree* with much of the alternative conception. That is, many theists are inclined to suggest that science does not give a complete account of the world, and that for a more ultimate or "meta-scientific" account one must move to a theistic position. However, theists who adopt the standard conception are inclined to say that in order to describe and explain the world at a meta-scientific level, one must say that there is *a being*, that is, God, who is the causal, intentional, source of the world. And, instead of proposing merely that there are certain meta-scientific divine principles or laws, advocates of the standard conception are inclined to insist that the being, God, has certain attributes or properties, by virtue of which the world may be more adequately described and explained. In other words, the standard conception affirms everything the alternative conception affirms, and then adds something more – the notion of God as a being.

Some readers may raise the following objection against the alternative conception. It seems the alternative reduces God to an idea. If God is not an entity that exists (or at least, could exist) then, isn't it the case that "God" is "just an idea" – a "philosopher's God" so to speak? How does this alternative count as true-blooded theism and not as a "demythologized" version of religion, far removed from traditional, good old-fashioned theism?

In a sense, the alternative could indeed be taken to say that the essence of

God is "just an idea." However, there is also a sense in which saying this would be misleading. On the alternative conception, a theist is committed to a certain view about *how the world works*, for he proposes that there are certain underlying structural principles in accord with which the world operates. He also considers that those principles are themselves explicable (up to a point) by reference to the necessary features of Being. The structural principles are "true" (or perhaps better: we can formulate true propositions which describe those principles); those principles (or propositions) are as true or real as say, the laws of gravity and the laws of chemistry and physics. Furthermore, the theist conceives of those divine principles as structurally more fundamental than the scientific principles. Since those principles have their explanatory ground in features of Being, it is therefore misleading to say that, on the alternative approach, Being, that is, God, is "just an idea" – as if that notion had no ramifications for what goes on in the world.

Furthermore, as explained earlier,[2] the alternative conception can provide an account of revelation, divine reward and punishment, prophecy, divine communication, and so on. In short, the alternative conception is *not* a version of deism. To be sure, the account of personhood and personality on the alternative conception *differs* from the account on the standard conception. But, as argued earlier, there is no explanatory or pragmatic loss in that account. Hence there is no reason to prefer the standard account on this score.

Another potential criticism against the alternative conception stems from the biblical language used to talk about God. This objection holds weight especially for those who take the Bible as a sacred text, which is true for many if not most theists today. Doesn't the Bible talk about God as an entity? The standard conception fits naturally into the way the Bible talks about God; the alternative seems rather removed from the plain meaning of the Bible.

However, this objection can be handled by saying that the Bible speaks in a commonsensical way about God that even a child can understand on some level. Most theists agree that the Bible uses anthropomorphic and anthropopathic language to describe God; that does not mean that at a philosophical level this needs to be interpreted literally. As is well known, the Bible itself endorses the view that God is radically different from all else, including humans.[3] Such biblical passages force us to take the anthropomorphic and anthropopathic passages with more than a grain of salt.

Following Maimonides and others, a rather convincing case can be made for the necessity of "different levels of discourse" about God. The advocate of the alternative conception need not deny the legitimacy, importance, and indeed pragmatic necessity of the standard conception of God – up to a point, that is, so long as it is understood as remaining at a certain level of discourse. That is, on one level of discourse, God may be spoken of and thought of as a being, with properties. Indeed, on one level of discourse, God is spoken of anthropomorphically and anthropopathically. Maimonides does not deny the usefulness, legitimacy, indeed necessity of this way of speaking about God, at least in some contexts. But on a deeper level of discourse, these forms of speech may not be the most accurate way of talking and thinking about God. After all, the Bible is not concerned to articulate a philosophically rigorous conception of God. That is the job of philosophers of religion, based of course on sacred texts, religious experience, and using the tools of logic and philosophical analysis.

The alternative conception has the following advantage over the standard conception. Someone who believes in God on the standard conception makes a much more grandiose ontological commitment than does someone who believes in God on the alternative conception. It follows that it would take much more to show that it is rationally defensible to have (even) a (minimal) belief in theism on the standard conception than on the alternative conception. Let us elaborate this point.

On the standard conception, God is a necessary being who is the causal source of the world, and who designed the world to have the structure and order which it has. As we saw above, this leaves the theist with several issues to address. First, we were left with a problem about how to understand God's necessity. If God is a being or entity, what *makes his existence necessary?* It is open for the anti-theist to challenge the coherence of the notion of a logically necessary (or "historically necessary") being. In addition, the prospects of constructing a rational defense for (even) a (minimal) belief in such a being are problematic. Of course, it would be presumptuous to deny the possibility that there might be some way of developing arguments to support this belief. Perhaps the ontological argument and the cosmological argument can be made to work. Or perhaps, the theist could argue that we know by divine revelation or religious experience that such a God exists. Indeed, this book has argued that religious experience does provide at least some minimal evidence for belief in God (Section 3.5). However, the door remains open for the skeptic to insist that no amount of religious experience can substantiate (even) a (minimal) belief in the existence of an entity or being that is *necessary*.

However, on the alternative conception, God is not conceived as a necessary *entity*; in fact, God is not an *entity* altogether. God's essence *just is* Being, in the abstract sense of the term. The account of God's necessity is rather straightforward; it is one with which many atheists will find themselves in agreement. All the metaphysical features of God (necessity, independence, eternality, uncreatedness, uniqueness) may be understood as aspects of Being. Additionally, on the alternative conception, God is not the causal source of all beings. Rather, God, that is, Being, is the ontological condition for all beings, in the sense that every being manifests or expresses Being. This too is something that even many atheists agree with, so long as Being is not "reified" into *a* being. And, it is precisely this reification that the alternative conception does *not* endorse.

The advantage of the alternative over the standard conception is not merely a matter of Ockham's razor, namely, that the alternative conception affirms less than the standard conception but with equal explanatory power. It is rather that on the alternative conception of God, it turns out many opponents of theism (that is, many atheists) *already accept* a good part of what theism seeks to affirm. On the alternative conception of God, part of the motivation for being an atheist (skepticism about the very notion of a necessary, non-spatial being that has properties and that acts) turns out to be irrelevant to the debate between theism and atheism.

Another advantage of the alternative conception is the following. Earlier we asked whether God's oneness or uniqueness follows from his necessity. If God is conceived as a being, it seems we could conceive the possibility that there be *many* essentially necessary realities. Some medieval philosophers tried to respond by arguing that only one necessary being could exist. But we can rule it out easily if God is conceived as *being itself*. For, Being is necessarily one, not multiple. (Actually the same is true for redness or triangularity. There are multiple red things and multiple triangles. But redness is what is, there aren't two "rednesses" unless one means to speak of two variations of redness, of course, which is a different matter.) Furthermore, God is not only one but unique (in a way that is *not* true of redness or triangularity). Nothing else is as primordial or foundational as Being itself.

Let us emphasize that on the alternative conception, theism does *not* collapse into making uninteresting or non-substantive claims about the world. Moreover, the difference between atheism and theism does not collapse. Rather, as stated earlier, the difference between theism and atheism will lie in profound differences over assertions about *how* the world is organized and structured; about such things as the fate and destiny of humankind. Certainly, the atheist will disagree with the theist's proposal that there are certain divine principles in accord with which the world is structured. And he will be skeptical about any arguments that seek to demonstrate or rationally substantiate (even) a (minimal) belief that such principles hold true.

Earlier we had claimed that many atheists *agree* that, in some sense, all things express Being, that Being is necessary, independent, and eternal, that Being is the necessary ontological condition for beings. However, with regard to God's personhood and personality the situation is different. The atheist has several options here. He can agree that Being is the ontological condition of all beings, but disagree that Being is in the above sense *free*. For he can make a sharp distinction between the claim that Being is the ontological condition of beings, which he agrees with, and the claim that Being is *supreme*, with which he does not agree. In effect this would be to disagree with the claim that the particular features of the world can be explained by appeal to features of being, in the way that the theist wishes to suggest. Or he can agree that Being is supreme and find some way to reject the argument given earlier linking supremacy to freedom and personhood. (The latter approach might be taken by the non-theistic Hindu, for example.)

Furthermore, on the alternative conception, there is no notion of God as the entity who designed and manages the world with benevolence and justice. Yet, on the alternative, theism maintains that the world has a certain moral structure or order, and that human destiny is shaped by that structure. Theism also holds that divine benevolence and divine justice are *true* principles. And with this the atheist will surely disagree. He will claim that there are no such principles. He will be skeptical about any attempt to provide reasons for believing that such principles are true. On this score, the alternative and the standard conceptions of God are equally distant from atheism.

In closing, it is important to re-emphasize that for the purpose of this book, it is not necessary to determine which conception of God's ontological status is more plausible. The reader need not agree with the conclusion of this appendix in order to accept the overall argument of this book.[4]

Notes

1   See Section 3.2, pp. 30–31.
2   Ibid., p. 44.
3   See, for example, Deuteronomy 4:12, Isaiah 55:8–9.
4   One more advantage is claimed for the alternative conception in Section 3.3.

Index